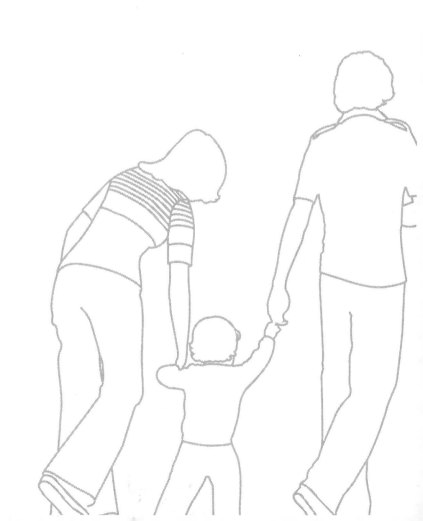

Published 2020
By Ryan Michael Painter

Cover design by Cindy Bean
Book design by Anita Boeira
Editing by Carolyn Janecek

ISBN: 978-1-7350512-0-8

credenda

plural noun

cre·den·da | \ krəˈdendə, krē'-\ : doctrines to be believed : articles of faith

WHEN DID YOU BECOME PHOTOGRAPHS?

When I think of my father, I never see him. I envision the rooms of his condo, the driver side seat where he sat, the little streams where the ducks would waddle and the greenhouse where the roses bloomed. He, an almost translucent creature who stands small and thin while lingering at the edge of life, before slipping from view. I could try and ad-lib his lines, but I've long since forgotten the sound of his voice and the dexterity of his vocabulary. For decades, I have looked with half-closed eyes, hoping to find him. He isn't in the leather chairs, the snow-painted Christmas trees, the empty Diet Dr. Pepper bottles, the hospital bed or the dust trapped in sunlight as it pours across these sterile locales. I've been caught in omniscient first person, a god exploring a museum world furnished with designer furniture, but the man who purchased and occupied these exhibits is no longer there.

It isn't that I am without a reference point. There are numerous photographs of my father. I even appear in the majority of them, as if to confirm that he and I were in these places that I remember as lifeless. But the photographs feel forged. I could cosmetically give him life: re-edit him into all the stages of my life and they'd feel as genuine as what is real. The shirtless man holding a baby, a toddler, a child, a teenager and reluctant adult. But I never could give him a smile; there is no record or memory of that.

I don't remember him breathing, what he smelled like, if his mustache brushed across my cheek when he kissed me good night, if when he combed my hair he was gentle, or if he were right or left-handed. There are crepe paper rainbows, a thumb-sucking gorilla and the stuffed clown he gave me that I accidentally saw in the walk-through closet between the den and the bathroom where he kept the water-filled milk jugs that he used as weights.

We are in his silver Mercedes, the top pulled back and the sun is bright and hot. We're turning out of his apartment complex; we're going east. My birthday is near; it must be the last week of May. I'm full of guilt having seen one of my presents. Had I wanted to? Was it an accident? Would he be angry? Did he start the conversation by innocently asking what I would want for my birthday or did I have my foot in my mouth before I even opened it? I've yet to learn how to be subtle, so dancing around the subject becomes a complete confession.

I don't remember his reaction; just the guilt. Was he disappointed that I wouldn't be surprised? Pleased that I was honest or worried that I couldn't keep secrets? Were there secrets to be kept? I can't see him. The sun is too bright, the trees too green against a sky too blue to ignore.

Michael, help me see you laughing. I can't even imagine it. I don't remember calling you Father or Dad. Just Michael—a name without a face, like God behind clouds, Neverland and Antarctica.

POSSESSION

In eighth grade, my English teacher, Mrs. Zimmerman, quietly convinced me that I had a talent for words, even if I couldn't spell them. This small, seeming insignificant moment would define me. I had by this point abandoned dreams of winning the World Series with the Los Angeles Dodgers and replaced them with a world that dazzled with Shakespeare's theatrics and the ringing of Johnny Marr's guitar. Writing fell within the image (i.e., outcast) I was cultivating, so it stuck. It would prove a lifesaver, not because it was easy, although I thought it was easier than it was, but because it was excruciating. I had yet to learn the value of words and spent them without concern for economy—recklessly writing epic poems with each break up, disappointment, and agitation. I was trying to keep my head from slipping beneath the water and writing proved to be a suitable floatation device.

I don't know when my mother started to press the idea, nor for how long the thought had been in her head, but by the time I reached the vast shores of university life, she started to encourage me to write about my childhood. Specifically, the time I spent with my father before he died of AIDS in 1983 when I was seven years old. I refused; it was her story to tell. I was too disorientated and waterlogged to see past the sensational aspects of the story. My father was Mormon and gay. Gay and Mormon. Never able to reconcile one with the other, he carried a sadness that I couldn't understand as a child. I didn't dare approach it as a young adult. What could I say that she couldn't say better? Truthfully, I was terrified that I would turn my father's struggles into tabloid fodder. I had no desire to capitalize on his sadness. Still, she insisted that it was my story, not hers.

In the late eighties, five or so years after my father's death, Mom read Mormon author Carol Lynn Pearson's *Goodbye, I Love You: The Story of a Wife, Her Homosexual Husband, and a Love Honored for Time and All Eternity* and corresponded through mail with Pearson about her own experiences. Pearson, who was one of the few outspoken Mormons who was openly sympathetic to the gay community during that era, asked her to "join the cause." Mom never cared much for the spotlight and politely declined Pearson's request. She knew that the story was incredibly important, but she also knew that I would be the one to tell it.

More than a decade after Mom made her first request, I finally relented and agreed to write this book. For the better part of two decades, I had carried my father's story inside of me. I rarely talked about it. It wasn't something I dared to mention in my teens, and as a young adult, I had my own struggles to contend with. It wasn't until my late twenties that my head dipped beneath the clouds and I began to see the world around me with a sense of clarity. I found myself surrounded by numerous friends that desperately, for many different reasons, needed to hear about my childhood.

So, I started talking. It was just a whisper; it felt like a scream. Twenty years after his death, I was finally able to begin to acknowledge the love I felt for my father. This newfound openness was liberating at first. In time, it asked me to reconsider even the smallest of details in my life. I had believed that my childhood was unremarkable.

I was wrong. I usually am.

METHOD AMONGST MADNESS

Following a string of incidents during my freshman year at Brigham Young University, a police officer was assigned to specifically keep an eye on the second and third floors of the W Hall dormitory. While I will admit we were a bit riotous, particularly considering the conservative nature of the school, the vast majority of us were not immoral by any standard. Nonetheless, Officer Wayne was often there to remind us that it was far easier for him to write a first-person report than to try and get statements from witnesses, so we might as well save him the work and invite him to come along on our next nefarious adventure.

Trying to reconstruct the past based on my memories is a difficult task. As a child, I didn't understand life enough to have any sense of what events would be important to tell my family's story. I held on to what felt important at the time. I could only riddle out a framework from these orphaned memories.

So, here I am, playing the role of Alice caught in the vestibule of Wonderland without any magical aid to get me through the tiny door that stands six-inches high and two-inches wide before me. There is a world full of exquisite detail on the other side. I know this because I was once on the opposite side, wondering when I'd get big enough to leave all of this childhood nonsense behind.

Perhaps, if I could only see my childhood as an adult, I could swap out my jumbled collection of smells, textures, and sights for concrete facts. But I was just a little boy who dreamed of wielding a lightsaber. I didn't suspect that I was living an extraordinary storyline that would someday be worth sharing.

Thankfully, my mother, aided by a journal that she kept between 1980 and 1984, helped map out my path to the past. I went through the wardrobe towards the streetlamp and beyond into the wilderness. I expected paradise; I found an escapeless maze of barbs, thorns, and rejection letters. So, I set up camp, closed my eyes, and dreamed of a place where storytelling was no longer necessary.

We might get there. We haven't arrived yet.

Sisyphus pushed his rock; Christ wandered the desert, and I, bound by reluctance and fear, kicked against the pricks. The only way forward was through the briar.

For the better part of a decade, I could tell my mother's half of the tale, but had avoided trying to understand my father's part in this story. Not because it is impossible to speak for the dead, but because I was afraid of what I might find if I dusted off my father's shoes and walked the streets of his past.

There is darkness. But where there is love, there is also light.

So, close your eyes and let it be a Technicolor dream that you see before you as the curtain rises. A vivid vision slightly out of focus, the colors emphasized over shape.

EMANATING STAR

It begins with a flood.

Between April and June 1952, the Missouri River rose above its levees and dikes, flooding the Midwest and displacing over 100,000 people. Volunteers, troops, and members of the Red Cross were called upon to build refugee camps, as well as strengthen and extend levees in hope of maintaining the river. It was in the shadows of this event that my mother, Patti Lee, was born to Jack and Beverly Young.

She was the first of seven children, six girls and a boy. Her earliest days were spent in Creighton and then Chadron, Nebraska, before settling in Riverton, Wyoming. Minus getting lost in a snowdrift, a tumble down a staircase, an incident involving a toad in a drawstring purse, and a case of measles, she had a fairly unremarkable childhood.

My mother was shy, but smart and always the best-dressed wallflower at dances. In high school, she busied herself with cheerleading, Concert Choir, and Thespian Club. She even made a run at being Homecoming Queen. The only thing that differentiated my mother from thousands of other All-American girls was that her family were members of The Church of Jesus Christ of Latter-Day Saints. Which, regardless of what you might have heard, isn't that different at all.

It wasn't until after high school that my mother began to discover she was more mystical, precious, and rare than her simple upbringing suggested. It started the summer before college, when she worked for Keebler setting up enticing displays and restocking the local grocery stores with cookies and delicious treats.

I realize the odds are that my mother didn't run around as Tinker Bell or one of Santa's little helpers. She probably wasn't dressed in a long red tunic with a giant black belt and green tights accompanied by pointed boots and a hat that drooped because of the oversized bell attached at the top; in my mind she does. Beautiful and full of magic, like an ambassador from Wonka's world, she swoops into supermarkets and entrances a small army of children with her basket of cookies, leading them blissfully away into a sugar-fueled heaven.

Even now, if you look closely as she rubs flour on the kitchen counter and rolls out cookie dough before cutting it into hearts, snowmen, ghosts, shamrocks, and stars, you'll catch a hint of her ability to turn the mundane into something wonderful. It only takes a little frosting and a cinnamon smile.

In my heart I believe someday I will round the corner, start into an aisle and find a young woman, small with soft features and rosy cheeks. She'll smile, pull one last box from her basket, place it on the shelf, look to me, nod with a wide smile and a wink to extenuate the twinkle in her eye just as she evaporates away leaving me warm and in love.

SMILE FOR THE CAMERA

For years, I was comfortable not knowing.

That goes for pretty much anything and everything related to my father, outside of my own memories. I imagined a future where I would be stronger, more able to confront whatever my father's past might be. It would be called *Excavating Michael*, an excursion that could compliment this text. It would have all the answers, none of the loose ends.

It didn't occur to me that Grandma Gloria and Grandpa Bob would die, that they would leave having never shared their memories and truths about their son, my father. There were times where I wanted to ask, but in their presence the request felt inconsiderate. I don't know that we ever spoke of him at all. He just lingered silently, beneath every breath.

I have a handful of photos of Michael from his youth. They arrived in a letter sent by Grandpa Bob's second wife, Joy, who never knew my father and as such, the photos have little to no context. They seem to be from random, unimportant, and shy childhood moments. In a few of the photos, my father wears an oversized suit coat with sleeves that entirely cover his hands. His eyes are bright and his smile is wide. A grin, unburdened by ghosts and secrets.

Among the photos is also a curiously staged image from my parents' wedding. Michael stands rigidly next to his father who looks happy, perhaps relieved, for his son. My father, for his part, looks like a man contemplating the end of the world.

LEFT UNSAID

Before he died, Grandpa Bob wrote his life story down for his grandchildren.

When he gave it to me, he pulled me close and said, "There are things I left out."

My father appears in two paragraphs.

> *I worked at the U of U for over two years. During this time there were two more memorable events in our family. Our second daughter arrived on April 12, 1948 and we named her Dawn Michelle Painter. Dawn sort of signifies the start of a new day of new life, and Michelle is the feminine version of Michael which we both liked very much. Then almost exactly a year later, our first son arrived on April 23, 1949. We named him Robert Michael Painter. Robert after me of course, and Michael because I have already stated we liked it a lot.*

And then ten pages later.

Mike received his Master's degree from the University of Utah. He Fulfilled a mission to Montreal, Quebec, Canada mission. He was an accomplished pianist. He married Patty Young in the Salt Lake Temple, later divorced. One child, Ryan. He was Contracts Administrator for Mountain Fuel Supply Company. Mike became very ill, was in the hospital twice, died of Respiratory Failure on September 19, 1983. He was only 43.

My mother's name is misspelled. My father was thirty-four when he died. These errors could suggest a certain laziness or carelessness, a disregard for the details. I believe that my grandfather wrote the paragraph and quickly moved on, never returning to proofread what had been the hardest sentences he had ever written.

THE ABSENTEE FATHER

Even after talking to some of my father's siblings and friends who knew him as a boy and in high school, the person they called Mike remained an enigma.

I can tell you that he was the third of six children, three girls and three boys. The first four children were born between 1945 and 1951. The last siblings were not born until 1958 and 1960. His early years were spent in Murray, a suburb of Salt Lake City, Utah. Bob was often away; he had the habit of going back to school or taking positions that severely limited his time with his family. This left Gloria alone to tend to the children. Gloria wasn't an ideal mother. My father's older sisters, Lynne and Dawn, were often sent to stand outside on the porch, sometimes alone and other times together, while their mother made, or pretended to make, phone calls to see if anyone would take them, because she didn't want them anymore. When night came, Gloria would call them back inside, "No one else wanted you either, go to bed."

By all accounts, Mike and his younger brother Les were treated less harshly.

There is a story that someone had gotten into the chocolate chips that were stored on a top shelf in the basement. Gloria was furious, lined up the four children, made them bend over with their palms against the floor and spanked them one by one until someone confessed.

Mike took the blame and the last spanking. He hadn't been the one to indulge on the sweets, Dawn had.

Les has kinder memories of playing with Mike in their grandparents' orchards, racing in a soapbox car that had the advantage of ten-inch ball-bearing wheels and watching matinee movies at the Villa Theater.

My father contracted polio when he was seven-years-old. His siblings don't remember much, except that his absence lasted for a few weeks.

In 1959, Bob and the family moved to Bad Vibel, a German town just outside of Frankfurt. My father took piano lessons and often played at church meetings. After three years, the family moved back to their home in Utah.

In high school, my father joined just about every club he could find, served as Senior Vice President, and was generally liked. He told Mom that he had also been a cheerleader. This was not true. For years, I thought that I had broken some family line, a birthright that I refused to embrace, by lettering in theater and writing on the literary staff.

His best friend, Steve, describes him as "conservative," "serious," and "spiffy." If there's one thing everyone agrees on, it is that Mike was well dressed.

During their senior year, Steve and my father often double dated. Steve frequently took Kay, a woman who would later become his wife. My father saw someone named Becky.

A MOST PECULIAR PEOPLE

Members of The Church of Jesus Christ of Latter-Day Saints (LDS, for brevity's sake), more commonly known as Mormons (a colloquial name once embraced, but now rejected, that I use with affection, rather than disdain), have the reputation of being a very odd group of people. This is partly self-assigned, but is also because members of the LDS faith are often confused as having traits that belong to the Jehovah's Witnesses, the Amish, or the Fundamentalist Church of Jesus Christ of Latter-Day Saints, a group that holds onto long abandoned traditions.

Let me assure you, Mormons like to dance, make use of electricity, and celebrate holidays. They aren't limited to wearing clothing inspired by *Little House on the Prairie*. They do their best to not smoke, drink alcohol, or have premarital sex. Once upon a distant time long, long ago, they practiced polygamy. They don't anymore.

That being said, there are some things that you'll need to know to understand some of the elements that influenced the course of this particular story.

From the earliest of ages, members of the LDS church are taught that the most important thing a person can do in this life is to get married and have a family—the more nuclear the better.

Having completed high school, my mother would have been expected to find a nice and faithful Mormon husband within a year or two and start having children. In netherworld of the late '60s and early '70s, women weren't encouraged to attend college. My grandmother, being a well-educated woman herself, insisted that my mother include college in her plans.

After high school, my father would have been expected to serve a two-year proselytizing mission for the church in some exotic place like Buenos Aries, Edinburgh, or Philadelphia. Upon returning, his suggested course of action would be to marry, finish university, and find a well-paying job that allowed him to provide for his dozen or so children. Well, maybe half a dozen children.

THE GREAT ESCAPE

In 1970, Mom set aside her elven ways to attend Brigham Young University in Provo, Utah. Her parents disapproved because BYU had the reputation of being less academic and more of a springboard for young Mormon girls to get married and drop out before graduation. Appropriately, my mother's counselor suggested she not worry about picking a major because she was just going to get married anyway. Mom chose chemistry but would later change to microbiology.

The dating situation at BYU was chaotic. Culturally speaking, Mormons aren't supposed to date non-members. So, the freshman boys, many of whom had come from areas where there weren't many LDS members, were suddenly presented with amazing prospects. Taking to the situation with gusto, they would line up multiple dates with different girls for any given day. Lunch with one, dinner with another, and ice cream with someone else that night. Amidst the dating frenzy, Mom started seeing Lon, a "real California surfer," who was in the ROTC.

In spring, Mom's sister Jackie, who was one year younger, came down to attend a scholars' conference. Lon set Jackie up on a date with his roommate and the four of them set out to see a free movie in the Joseph Smith Building's auditorium. The auditorium's layout was essentially a large chapel designed for capacity and not comfort, with long pews that sat twenty people apiece and were spaced closely together so that there was very little legroom.

Upon arriving at the Joseph Smith Building, my mother learned that night's film was *Wait Until Dark*. Mom has always been restless when it came to films wrought with tension. She had seen the film twice before and dreaded the prospect of seeing it again. Waiting in line, she joked that it wasn't her favorite movie. Her hints, subtle or otherwise, went unnoticed.

As the movie began, my mother's tension kept escalating. Halfway through the film, at no particular climax of the storyline, she couldn't contain herself. The claustrophobia of the room combined with the building anticipation of what was to come in the film's narrative overwhelmed her. She stood up and started screaming. Caught in the middle of a row, she continued screaming until those around them filed out and let the four of them escape. Rushing outside, she relaxed in the fresh air, feeling a bit foolish and shocked by her own behavior.

At the end of the spring semester, Lon asked my mother to come visit him in California. Mom was afraid, not of Lon or meeting his family, but of California itself. California with its vast beaches, its glitz and glamour, seemed like a distant world with customs far removed from everything she knew. Even when her mother offered to pay for her flight, Mom refused to go.

MISSIONARY MAN

My father served his two-year mission for the LDS Church in Montreal, Canada.

I've been given a handful of letters that were written by my father to Steve, his best friend, who was serving in Germany during this period of their lives. In most of the letters, my father has ornate, perfectly spaced handwriting. There's a glorious, youthful positivity to them.

June 24, 1968

Thanks a lot for you and Kay seeing me off. It is really a weird feeling to wave goodbye to such good friends. The train ride was long (26 hours) and tiring but it gave me time to think (and get homesick). We had our first missionary experience on the train that night. About 10 of the [missionaries] sang hymns while touring the train cars. After singing for 2 hours we had quite an audience in each car. We explained who we were and what we were doing. We bore our testimonies and handed out some pamphlets and a few Book of Mormons.

July 15, 1968

Things are just tremendous. I have really been blessed. Guess what! I will have my first baptism July 27th. Isn't that something. We are baptizing a 22 yr old woman who is really golden. She came along just like a champ.

August 19, 1968

It sounds so different to see all of our friends going on missions, getting married etc. Boy, I guess we are finally growing up, huh Steve!?

Undated, Fall 1968

How is everything? I'm really proud of ya Steve, so keep up the good work and you'll be blessed for it. Missionary life is challenging and fabulous.

October 21, 1968

I sure have been blessed with people to teach and baptize. It is really wonderful to be an ambassador for our Father in Heaven. Out of all the billions of people in the world we are two out of 13,000 chosen and ordained to spread the word of God here on the earth. Boy what a responsibility and a blessing. I about cry every time I think of the love our Father in Heaven has for us.

Becky appears, but only in the sense that my father saw little reason to hold onto any notion that their relationship would continue after his mission.

October 21, 1968

> *I haven't heard from Becky for 2 months. I feel real bad but I can't let it affect my mission. I have written her 4 times in hope that she will answer but I guess she knows what she wants. I probably deserve it anyway.*

In the same letter, my father had a far more optimistic opinion of Steve and Kay's chances.

> *I think it is wonderful that Kay is helping you so much. She really is some girl. If you fulfill an honorable mission, doing all in your power to serve our Father in Heaven (which I have full trust you will) Kay will be waiting for you. Our Father in Heaven knows what is best for us and if you serve Him, He will bless you in many ways. Kay would be one of those blessings.*

Steve is convinced that my father was more than a little sweet on Kay; she disagrees. In every letter my father wrote to Steve she is mentioned, even if only as a postscript.

There are two letters, one at the very end of his mission and another written after he had come home, where the script is in cursive and rushed. The wistful tone replaced by the uncertainness that comes when the future is less scripted.

June 6, 1970

> *Germany must be beautiful this time of year, probably much like Canada. I love Canada and the people here but the inevitable is soon approaching. I plan on being released June 19 and then working the summer. Perhaps a few trips to Mexico via California and a few other places will take place but everything is so undefined.*

Undated, Summer 1970

Oh Steve, there has been so much going on and so many changes in the both of us a letter hardly begins to express anything. I will just have to wait.

I don't want to "freak" you out because I know how you love your mission. I too hated to leave and I am very homesick for Canada. It will be really great to enjoy your friendship again and I know that both our testimonies have grown so much.

O CANADA

Missions are strange, intimate, and unique experiences. One day, you are carefree and young and then you wake and find yourself in a distant, foreign place with strangers for companions. You try to be selfless and confident, but most days foolhardy will have to do.

You move from street corners to porches and the occasional living room, having conversations that reveal parts of yourself that you've only just discovered in the moment.

It was one of the loneliest periods of my life. My insides still twist at the thought of it. It's ridiculous that decades later, the vulnerability remains.

It is incredibly difficult for me to think about how my father might have felt on his mission without being blinded by the sorrow of my own atypical experiences.

I've always wondered when he recognized he was gay. Did he live in denial, burying his attractions beneath his beliefs? Was he bewildered, unable to decipher what he felt?

The first time I read my father's letters to Steve, I wanted to dismiss his enthusiasm as a smokescreen, a bit of frosting heavily applied to hide what was beneath the surface. Because it would be easier to believe that my father had accepted his sexuality and had decided to live a double life. That would relieve him of the struggle between faith and feeling. He'd be a great pretender, rather than a young man adrift in spiritual crisis.

I found on my mission that while the body is given a strict regimen, the mind tends to roam free. Introspection is encouraged and prayers are as common as punctuation. You wake, you pray. You shower, you pray. You eat, you pray. You teach, you pray. You serve, you pray. At the end of the day you collapse into sleep as you pray.

In the reverent silence, every doubt and uncertainty festers. You begin to question your ability to do the work at hand. Are you worthy to be a representative of Christ or are you a charlatan, masquerading behind a feigned piety?

Had Michael come to Canada to serve God or to find a reprieve?

CUPID'S FOLLY

In the fall of 1971, Mom returned to BYU and lived off campus with her sister Jackie. Most of the boys her age were either on missions or attending classes until they turned nineteen. Mom's boyfriend Lon was to leave for his mission in October but came to Provo to work the couple months before he left. The spark was gone and he and Mom agreed to start seeing other people.

That's when Ralph made his entrance. Ralph was smooth, well-connected, and wide in stature. He was the life of the party, the funny guy who everyone loved—except my mother.

Their relationship started, and should have ended, with a miserable blind date. But Ralph showed up on her doorstep a few days later, claiming to have had a "vision" in which God told him that she was supposed to be his wife.

Mom did her best to avoid him, but it proved impossible to escape from someone who knew and was known by everyone. Soon, she was his guilty-by-association girlfriend.

The day before Mother's Day, Ralph came begging with a diamond ring. His father had proposed on Mother's Day and it would be a special surprise to his mom if he brought his new fiancée with him to church the following day. Mom reluctantly agreed. Upon arriving at church, Ralph proceeded to introduce her to the entire congregation as "the mother of his children." Mom promptly returned the ring and went into hiding for the last two weeks of the semester.

Her first night back in Wyoming, Mom attended a church activity with her family only to watch in disbelief as Ralph waltzed into the cultural hall. He proceeded to flash his charm and announced that he and my mother were going to get married. Yet again, Mom disagreed with his prediction. This was followed by the unexplainable: Ralph confidently strode away from the church and danced out of my mother's life completely.

COURSEWORK

Based on the letters, Steve wanted Mike to attend Brigham Young University with him after they both completed their missions.

October 21, 1968

> *I have been thinking about what you said about going to the Y. I really would like to Steve. I guess I will just have to pray about it. It is really wonderful and comforting to know that the Lord will answer our prayers.*

Eighteen or so months later, the idea of attending BYU made its way back into the conversation.

> *I have been accepted at BYU (which now days is quite an accomplish-*
> *ment) and I am seriously considering going there. I pray my finances will*
> *enable me to, if not I will go to the U for a while.*

It didn't happen.

Mike ended up attending the College of Business at the University of Utah.

ONCE MORE WITH FEELING

For Sadie Hawkins, Jackie, the most socially aware of the sisters, set my mother up with Nick, a disillusioned microbiology major. He and my mother dated the remainder of the semester. Near Christmas, Nick's mother became very ill with a rare blood disease. Returning to California for the Christmas break, Nick decided to stay at home, work, help take care of his mother, and figure out what he wanted to do with school.

In Nick's absence, my mother started dating Hal, a graduate student she knew from one of her labs. In spring, Mom returned to Wyoming and worked in a drug store until her internship at LDS Hospital in Salt Lake City, Utah, started in June. Nick wrote with news of his imminent return to Provo where he was going to finish up his degree and then apply to law school. With this news, my mother told Hal that their relationship had reached its end.

In June, she moved to Salt Lake City where she lived in a light and airy house that had been split into thirds and converted into apartments. That summer, Nick would come up to see her as often as his schoolwork allowed. By July, he started to talk about getting married. My mother was hesitant. Nick was persistent and began to tell people that they were going to get married. My mother would jokingly respond, "Married? But we're not even engaged!"

Soon, Nick presented my mother a card that read, "This is the last straw." Included in the card was a bunch of straw. Attached to one was a little plastic bag. In the bag was a diamond. She gleefully accepted. Nick pushed for a December wedding. Overwhelmed by her internship and the prospect of having to plan a wedding, Mom asked if they could hold off until the following summer. Nick insisted on December.

THE IMMEASURABLE DISTANCE BETWEEN

In July of 1973, the LDS Church decided to organize a "singles ward" in the downtown area of Salt Lake City. This would be a special congregation made up of young single adults who had managed to graduate from college without getting married. Anyone who wished to attend would need to be interviewed by his or her current bishop.

Not wanting to attend church with a congregation of older adults and married couples, my mother went to be interviewed. Having just moved into the area in June, my mother's bishop didn't know her at all. He ran her through a thorough interview and grilled her about her relationship with Nick. She admitted that she was attracted to him. This caused the bishop to jump to the conclusion that pre-marital sex was about to take place and that she needed to break off the engagement and wait for someone who would share their first kiss over the altar like he and his wife had.

Between the bishop's advice and Nick's unwillingness to delay the wedding, my mother broke off the engagement.

Over the years they would keep tabs on each other through Jackie and other intermediates. Nick would graduate from law school and marry a girl from Idaho Falls. He moved to Colorado where he died in his sleep ten or so years later of an undiagnosed tumor.

I remember the day Mom found out quite vividly. I was sitting on her bed. She was in front of the mirror getting ready to rush off to one place or another. She was on the telephone with one of her sisters when everything went silent. Hanging up the phone she didn't say much and tried to hide the pain. She was devastated—hurt in a way I had never witnessed and haven't seen since. What was wrong? A friend had died.

Now I understand. No, not a friend; a "what if?"

MAN & WOMAN

In the wake of breaking off the engagement with Nick, Mom dated a few people but nothing serious developed. In spring of 1974, she had mono and struggled through to finish her internship and graduate from BYU. The hospital, pleased with her performance, hired her. Her new shift had her working seven days on and seven days off from 5 a.m. to 3:30 p.m.

My mother doesn't remember meeting Mike. She knew he was in the Elders Quorum Presidency, a very respectable church position, and knew his roommate Jon fairly well because they worked together in the Sunday School at church. Sometime in May, Jon came to deliver something to my mother and Mike tagged along. As they arrived, a young man was leaving my mother's apartment in disgust. He greeted them by saying, "She's all yours if you want her." He had taken my mother out a few times and the relationship wasn't progressing as planned. Jon was quick to depart, leaving Mike to linger and cough nervously through small talk before asking her out to a movie the following weekend. It would have been rude to not accept.

Convinced that she was taller than him, my mother made sure to wear the flattest shoes she owned. He picked her up in his red VW Bug and took her to the Villa movie theater. There was a large crowd outside and Mike moved quickly through it, leaving her behind. She reached to take his hand, but on contact, he immediately jerked it away. She felt reprimanded, but perhaps she had been too forward. They saw the film adaptation of the Broadway musical *Mame* starring Lucille Ball, Bea Arthur, and Robert Preston. He was taller than she had remembered him being.

That summer, Mike graduated from the University of Utah and was hired by Northwest Energy Corporation as a contract administrator. He was fortunate to get the job because it was typically given to a lawyer, but a court ordered break up of Energy Corporation into smaller companies initiated a mass hiring and they were willing to train him on the job. He purchased a condo in a new development south of Salt Lake that would be completed at summer's end.

My mother continued to date him the rest of the summer. The relationship was awkward. He was always nervous, coughed a lot and never touched her. Still, he was kind and worked around my mother's schedule that required her be home early and made few demands. He didn't seem to mind and would just go and do something else after dropping her off at home. Jon was getting married in August, so he moved out of Mike's apartment. Carlton, a friend who had a photography business, became the new roommate.

While Mike's detachment had made their relationship easy, his distance robbed it of its comfort and left her feeling unattractive. Not wanting to appear forward, she built up the courage to ask him why he hadn't held her hand or tried to kiss her. He explained that it had always been his goal to kiss his wife for the first time over the altar. It sounded sweet, more romantic than anything he'd said before. It, of course, also reminded her of the advice she had been given a year before. But was he attracted to her? No, he said, he wasn't. Not nearly as sweet or romantic, simply confusing.

GHOSTLY

"He was a haunted man." These are the words that stay with me; it is the only truth I know for certain. In the happiest of memories, my father seems distracted. In photos, he seems divided, eyes staring off into bleakness. Maybe this is a result of his absence. My mother and I speak of him like a stranger, the constant unraveling of details and ideas as steppingstones leading to an unattainable understanding. In these moments, as the truth evaporates, leaving only guesswork and conjecture, her face pales and her eyes focus elsewhere, searching for a new detail in a face she has not seen for decades; always finding only one adjective: haunted.

THE PAINTER FAMILY (AS EXPLAINED BY MY MOTHER)

Mike's family lived across the street from a country club and owned a fleet of VW Bugs. The Painters weren't high society, but Mom worried that she and her family came across as backwoods hicks. The perceived distance between the families' classes didn't come up in conversations; it lingered like a Dickinsonian plot device.

The Painters were Mormon, active in the church and appeared to be nothing short of typical. Gloria, Mike's mother, worked in the medical field. Bob,

Mike's father, had wanted to be a doctor, but Gloria didn't want to endure medical school, so he became an accountant with the government.

Gloria loved to plan parties and would insist on doing all of the cooking and preparation after which she would be too exhausted to come and enjoy the time with her family. Mom believes that her approval was extremely important to Mike. She had been told that Mike recently dated a girl he had met while doing some modeling, presumably for his roommate Carlton or one of his many photographer friends. The model had failed to live up to Gloria's expectations—not a good Mormon girl. So, she was unceremoniously dismissed by Mike as an inappropriate smokescreen. My mother, however, seem to fit the bill. Mormon, successful, and malleable enough to mold.

PAINTING THE ROSES RED

My mother was invited by her bishop to attend a summer party and could "bring a date if she could find one." Immediately, he was apologetic for his poor choice of words. My mother explained she had been dating Mike all summer and would come with him. He was surprised, but pleased, to hear that they were dating.

The last week of August, Mike called and asked my mother to go to dinner on Saturday night. There was a formality in his request that caused her to panic. Despite the emotional divide that existed between them, she knew he was going to propose. Scrambling, she pointed out that the following day would be the first Sunday of the month and, as is the Mormon tradition, she intended on starting her twenty-four-hour fast that evening. So dinner wouldn't work. He insisted on seeing her.

He showed up with a dozen red roses and they walked the few blocks to Temple Square where he proposed.

I really could not think of a reason not to marry him. He had a good job, active church member, an almost finished condo, I had graduated from college... Did I love him? I didn't think that he had ever let me close enough to find out. I had been engaged a few times before and my family was sure I was never going to go through with it. Jackie had gotten married in June. I couldn't see a good reason why not.

Spencer W. Kimball, the President of The Church of Jesus Christ of Latter-day Saints during this time frame, believed that "almost any two good people can get along together and be reasonably happy together if both are totally cooperative, unselfish and willing to work together." It was, and continues to be, a fairly common ideology amongst Mormons. My mother insists that this way of thinking had little to do with her decision to get married. It would, however, influence her behavior down the road.

A DAILY EXISTENCE

Every morning, I wake up in the shadow of my father and mother's past. A lovely metaphor, but in this case, it is quite literal. Half a block to the west of my tiny apartment is the building where my father worked. I remember visiting him only once. His office was small and not luxurious like those on television. There was a picture of me and nothing else on the traditionally sterile desk. A block to the east was my father's favorite furniture store which closed when the economy swept it, and many other local businesses, under the carpet. While it was still open, I would pass by daily, looking in at the exaggerated elegance of the purposely-artful furnishings and could imagine my father picking out the gaudy stuffed quail that hung above his fireplace among the period pieces. I never went in. It was too much like a film set: so many knickknacks carefully placed to suggest that a life could actually exist there, even though it never has. For a time, it was simply one of many empty spaces waiting to be filled. A consulting firm, whatever that might be, cheaply remodeled the exterior. I'd mortgage my life to own it if I thought any part of my father remained there.

Two blocks away is the house where my mother lived when she and my father first met, his apartment is equally as close. I've walked past my mother's place once, set out one evening when I should have been writing, but had so little to say. It was dark; the house revealed no secrets.

Long gone are the Blue Mouse, an art house theater with a somewhat seedy reputation, and the alternative bookstore, Cosmic Airplane. There's a nice coffee shop now. Its windows fog up in the wintertime as young people sip hot drinks and wander outside to smoke a cigarette.

For a couple years, I attended church in the same building where my parents' paths originally intersected. I wish I could report that I found their names carved into the back of one of the pews in the balcony that looks over the chapel. I would have found comfort in tracing "Michael hearts Patti" a thousand times and never would have grown tired of the romantic nostalgia. There was no romance, nothing to immortalize in the heavily lacquered wood.

I thought that he had loved her, that she was taken in by his warmth and charm. I wanted to believe that God would have given her that much. Instead, she was offered struggle and cold distance from the first moment. It begs the question: why would anyone marry someone they didn't love?

THE RELUCTANT GROOM

The day after Mike proposed, everyone at church was delighted to learn of the engagement. A visit with Leland Davey, Mike's mission president in Canada, was reassuring and silenced the lingering doubts within my mother. Mike had served as President Davey's assistant for a fair share of his mission and had developed a close bond with him and his wife. They loved him dearly.

My mother started on the wedding plans. They set the date as November 22nd. Mike's roommate Carlton took the engagement photos and the invitations were sent out. She saw very little of Mike as he busied himself by furnishing the condo. When she did see him, he only wanted to talk about money and was critical of the amount she was spending on the wedding, repeatedly telling her that his sister had bought a washer for her new house when she got married rather than wasting it on a reception.

Mike moved into the condo in October and my mother saw even less of him. He told her Kent, an old friend from Germany, had just moved to town and wanted to spend some time with him before they got married. There were showers to attend, last minute details and work to keep her busy. The red flags went unnoticed. Lost, she and Mike looked to Gatsby's flashing light on the horizon.

The night before the wedding, my parents' families planned to meet and go to the Salt Lake Temple together. Early that morning, Mike called and said he didn't know if he could go through with the wedding. He canceled the honeymoon and still needed to spend some time with Kent. He reiterated that it wasn't her fault; he just wasn't attracted to her. He asked Patti to make a list of the wedding expenses. He would pay her back for whatever she had spent. Then, he wavered. He would call her back and let her know if they would go ahead with the wedding.

Dazed, Mom borrowed her roommate's car and drove to pick up Mike's ring.

Mom's family arrived from Wyoming late in the day. It was already time to go to the temple. Mike had not called. Mom was confused, moving towards panic. The wedding announcements had been sent; the wedding had to take place. In the stress of the moment, she let slip to her mom that Mike didn't find her attractive. Beverly was devastated. My mother calmed herself by rationalizing, "Why should he be attracted to me?"

Arriving at the temple, my mother was set aside to wait for Mike's arrival. She waited quietly. Hadn't she been faithful? Hadn't she done exactly what was asked of her? No Mike. Was she prepared to make this monumental decision? Going through the temple for the first time was a major commitment. How long could she wait? The temple workers suggested she go through without him. What choice did she have? She agreed and was placed with a group of young women who were about to become missionaries. She lost all connection with her senses. Her parents were there, but she could no longer make out their faces. She could only see herself kneeling at the altar, waiting for a man who would never arrive. On the eve of what was meant to be the crowning achievement of her life, she was alone.

Mike hadn't shown. His family was furious, hers bewildered.

Stepping through a curtain into a prayer room, my mother found Mike full of apologies. Something had come up and he needed to leave. He wasn't sure if he would be there tomorrow for the wedding. She should make a list of expenses. The numbness swelled around her.

The two families dissolved in confusion and strayed in opposite directions. Mom and her parents went to a nearby diner for a hamburger and then home. They ate in silence. Back at her apartment, her parents slept in her room while she lay awake on the couch until morning.

It was a grey, rainy day. The wedding was to be at 9 a.m. 9 a.m. came and went. The guests lingered in the silence, only occasionally whispering between themselves. There was no slipping in with the missionaries now. With no way to move forward alone, Mom prepared to escape just as Mike showed up. There was nothing that could be said. The apologies had run dry. They were married by President Davey in a room of light and mirrors. My mother remembers nothing of what was said—only that her new husband kissed her across the altar.

Carlton took their picture as they stood under a black umbrella in sheets of rain with the Salt Lake Temple lingering in the background.

Wet, exhausted, and confused, my mother crawled into Mike's red VW Bug, thankful to be out of the rain. He needed to pick up his tuxedo (in the temple he would have worn a simple white suit). They had agreed on black or grey, but he returned with light blue. She insisted it would clash with the forest green bridesmaids' dresses and dried yellow flowers. He brushed aside her complaint, saying he liked the blue better.

They arrived at his parents' for brunch. The house was incredibly dark. A few more pictures were taken at the condominium clubhouse where the reception took place. True to form, Gloria, Mike's mother, had made all of the desserts. My mother had made her own wedding dress; it wasn't fancy, but it was the most complicated dress she had ever made. She had spent the night worrying about what Gloria thought of it. Jackie was pregnant, her other sister, Terri, had just had surgery on her foot and needed some help getting around. Mike skirted around, accepting the congratulatory messages from the clueless guests and never took my mother's hand the entire evening.

That evening in their condo, he locked himself in the bathroom. My mother lay in the bed, alone. In the morning, they were to drive to Wyoming for another open house and then spend the night in a luxurious home that belonged to friends of her parents. At least her family would be at the reception. This would have been the happiest of her thoughts.

En route to Wyoming, Mike asked for an annulment. They both acted their role through the open house, although she still isn't sure why. They stayed the night but left the following morning without going to church with her family. Terrible weather delayed their return. By the time they got home it was late, too late to call President Davey and say they had made a mistake.

The call never was made.

HIS AND HERS

With just a door between them, my father sat in one hemisphere and my mother in another.

> *Our Father in Heaven knows what is best for us and if you serve Him, He will bless you in many ways.*

The cold, hard title. The emptiness of a half-filled bed.

> *I couldn't see a good reason why not.*

In those absent moments that surrounded my parents' wedding, my father was with Kent. I don't know the nature of their relationship. I don't even know if Kent was gay. Since learning my mother's side of the story in my late twenties, I've always assumed that Kent was my father's boyfriend. I imagined that the night before, he held Michael as he cried, agonizing over the uncertainty of what he should do.

This is the happiest version of the story that I can make.

If not lovers, perhaps Kent was a friend trying to keep someone he cared about from making a mistake. They were certainly tethered in some way. Kent had something to lose if my father went ahead with the marriage.

My father's decision to marry my mother can be viewed as an act of strength. It can also be read as a moment of weakness. Whatever existed between Kent and my father was more real than the relationship my parents shared.

SCENES FROM A MARRIAGE

Returning from Wyoming, the newlyweds were faced with the prospect of a week off and no honeymoon. It's possible that Mike had never planned one, which would have had made it easy to cancel. If he had planned one, Kent had talked him into canceling it.

Mom walked on eggshells as she went about moving into the condo and organizing the kitchen. This was made easy by the strange impracticality of the wedding gifts. No pots or pans, but expensive knickknacks aplenty. Mike said very little and avoided her by building a mock fireplace with Kent in the living room before moving on to installing shelves for the storage area.

The condo was ground-level, half buried in a hill with a little area in the back cut into the slope and braced by a railroad tie where you could plant a tiny garden. It was dark; sunlight only passing through the windows come mid-afternoon. The wall in the dining area was mirrored; the darkness seemed to go on forever.

Prior to this, my mother had never met Kent, but it turned out that she worked with his brother, Dan. Dan was older, bald, short, and very unusual. He helped the pathologists do autopsies and cleaned glassware. Everyone avoided him because he sold Amway and could talk for longer than anyone could listen. Kent looked nothing like his brother. He seemed kind.

For a while Mike would kiss her "hello" or "goodbye," making as little contact as possible. It wasn't long before he stopped making the effort. They shared a bed but kept to the edges. She wanted to be a wife. He didn't want to feel indebted. He wouldn't let her cook for him. He wouldn't let her wash his clothes or do his ironing. She could have the bedroom closet; he'd use the den where his clothes were arranged in categories and color themes and faced the same way. He had his bathroom; she had hers.

Having only one car flawed the complete separation. To ease Mike's burden, my mother arranged to split a seven on seven off shift with one of her co-workers, which meant she would work three days one week and four the next. Her shifts would begin at 7 a.m. and last until 5:30 p.m. On the days she worked, Mike would drop her off at the hospital and then go to Kent's house to get ready for work. After work, he would pick her up at the hospital. On the days she didn't work she was stuck at home. She wrote thank you notes, cleaned, cooked, anything to pass the time. She checked out books from the library—nothing particularly obscure, just your typical fiction. Mike came home and went through a few pages of one of the books. He said they were trash and returned them to the library.

Within the month, she would find multiple letters from Kent to Mike. Kent was furious with Mike for getting married. Risking an extended Amway pitch, she asked Dan about his brother. Yes, Kent and Mike had known each other in Germany, but he hadn't recently returned to Salt Lake. He had been back for nearly ten years.

FATHERLAND

When my father lived in Germany for three and a half years between 1959 and 1962, he would have been ten years old when he arrived, thirteen when he left. Kent was there; presumably they attended school, perhaps even church, together. Friends, living on the fringe of a new and uncertain world amongst the American outsiders in Germany's reconstruction after World War II.

It's a beautiful setting with a miniscule seed of truth. A foundation where you could parallel two young boys' coming of age against the landscape of a divided country searching for its own sense of self. Kent could be gentle and kind. Michael could be vulnerable and torn—still buoyed by a child's optimism and the secret of love shared between them.

OBSCURED BY INEXPERIENCE

The Stonewall riots of 1969 marked the beginning of the modern gay rights movement, but its reach was initially limited to major cities with established gay communities. In Middle America, gay culture existed, but it was closeted by a community effort to look the other way.

1969 was also the year that Fanfare Films released racing-driver-turned-movie-director Bruce Kessler's *The Gay Deceivers*. The film's plot is simple: two young men dodge the draft by pretending they are gay. When the recruiting officer doesn't buy into their ploy, the two young men are forced to take the charade to flamboyant heights.

The film is mediocre at best and would have made for a terrible crash course in how to spot a gay man with its reliance on stereotypes. It lacks the charm or the heart of a film like *La Cage aux Folles*, which wasn't released until 1978.

Mom knew nothing of Stonewall; she had seen *The Gay Deceivers*.

Mike had flamboyant aspects to his personality, but on the surface, he was just different from the other men she'd known. It never would have occurred to my mother that my father was gay, because Mormons weren't gay. It was inconceivable.

MERRY MISERY

Christmas was fast approaching, but Mike said that since they had just gotten married, no one would expect presents. She couldn't get him anything and he wouldn't be getting her anything. What could have been a joyous time was lost to the drabness of his indifference. It would be her first Christmas away from her family.

She spirited away some hope. No longer an intern, she would be getting a Christmas bonus. Someone the year before had commented that the bonus was nearly as big as their regular paycheck. Mom planned to use it to buy presents and surprise Mike on Christmas morning. Her Christmas bonus was twenty-five dollars.

On a snowy day in December, she walked to Cottonwood Mall to do some Christmas looking. It was a fairly long walk and nothing unusual happened, but when Gloria found out, she was furious. Didn't my mother realize that Ted Bundy was loose in Utah and that she fit the profile of his victims? Mom had to promise to stay in the shadowy confines of the condo and not to go out walking again.

Mom's efforts to be a dutiful wife during the holiday season were scorned by Mike, making Christmas particularly miserable. The unraveling situation worsened as my mother's back started hurting. An orthopedic surgeon gave her some anti-inflammatory and muscle relaxation medication. She went into work and took the medicine. She started to feel dizzy and her co-workers sent her to lie down. Five hours later, they woke her to go home.

It so happened that Jon, Mike's old roommate, and his wife, now pregnant, were visiting from Montana. Mike had invited them to come to dinner that evening. Fortunately, my mother had already prepared the majority of the meal and was finished cooking by the time they arrived. The medicine allowed her to relax. But relaxation, in this case, had a strange effect: she couldn't stop laughing. Jon had come to talk about the polygamous religion he and his wife had joined. Having been excommunicated from the LDS church, Jon vied for my mother and Mike's sympathy in hope of borrowing their temple recommends, which was their only hope of getting into the LDS temple. My mother's constant laughter undermined the conversation. Mike was furious. Jon and his wife left empty handed, belittling them for their narrow point of view.

KNOW YOUR PART

My mother received an invitation from her cousin Ted and his wife to attend a party at their house. She had only seen Ted a few times and when they arrived, there was a room full of people she didn't know and a "chef" cooking the group dinner. She was leery and as the evening progressed, it became clear that this was a sales party. Miracle Maid cookware, so good (and expensive) that it wasn't sold in stores (only at parties where you could be wined, dined, and pressured not only by the salesman, but by friends, family, and even strangers). The cookware was over two-hundred dollars. Mike signed up to buy the entire set. My mother was shocked. Weeks later, Mike complained about the extravagance of the purchase. She realized that he had expected her to play his mother's role and say he couldn't buy them.

To Miracle Maid's credit, my mother still has most of the set and frequently uses it. Not so extravagant after all.

AFTER A FASHION

Mike was a chameleon—constantly changing the way he dressed, depending on the friends he had. When they were first married, he wore knit dress shirts. Later, it was cowboy style clothes (for Kent), colored dress shirts, young people's clothes, a more mature wardrobe. Another time it was a vintage sailor suit (for a young mechanic married to a much older woman). My mother always knew something was going on when he bought new clothes.

One night, Mike returned home from work with some clothes for her. One of the girls in his office had worn the outfit. Having never met the woman, my mom believes she had probably been the tall and thin sort. Mom was thin, but not tall, and the outfit didn't fit her in the same way. She asked if she could return it and get something she'd look better in. Mike was disappointed.

CIRCUMSTANCE

Despite the increasing void between them, my parents continued to attend church together on a weekly basis. Mike refused to go to the temple with my mother, but she continued to go once a month. When Mom was asked to work with the teenage girls at church, Mike was very supportive. It gave him time to do whatever he wanted. One evening, upon returning home from an activity with the girls, she found the condo dark. It was late and she thought Mike must be asleep, so she quietly went in. Suddenly, a man came rushing past her and out the door. Mike accused her of spying on him. Frustrated, he told her his father had never accepted him and that it was important for him to have male friends. My mother remembers this as the moment when he confessed his attraction to men, but when she brought it up later, he would say she was jumping to conclusions.

But conclusions were not hard to jump to. No longer blinded by her naïveté, Mom couldn't help but start noticing that when they were out together, Mike would run into people he knew and they would agree to meet later. He tried to do so subtly; he would take my mother home first and then disappear. Sometimes, he had an excuse and other times he didn't bother. The curtains had been thrown open and all that remained was facing the frigid truth.

He still spoke of annulment—certain that he had made a mistake.

Mom believes that above all else, it was his desire to have a son that drove Mike to marry her. There may have been a deal with God, marriage as a peace offering, or one last attempt to please his mother, but the idea of a son was what saw it through. He had long since chosen a name, Jason, and bought furniture in preparation of his birth. But Jason would require something of him that he was not prepared to do. He had to decide what he wanted more: divorce or a son.

In the spring, Mike bought a yellow Opal GT and gave my mother the red VW Bug. The freedom pushed them further apart.

UNIMMACULATE

Ten months after the wedding, it was decided. Mike wanted a son regardless of what it would take. He asked my mother to determine when she was most fertile and he would be willing to try. She determined the date, they tried, he hated it, and it would never be done again. The first time was the last time. She was pregnant.

Alas, the pregnancy did not bring any majestic change to the marriage. My mother was tired and sick and slept as often as possible. Mike's initial happiness and relief was quickly muted as he dove into his own depression. The idea of having a son had propelled him through the darkness, but now that a child was on its way, he could no longer see where life was heading.

Even in his misery, it was necessary now more than ever, that the sadness be masked by a guise of normality. To celebrate their first wedding anniversary, Mike invited his parents over and presented my mother with a dozen roses and a grandfather clock. The clock, like the majority of the gifts he gave my mother, was impractical, expensive, and the sort of thing he'd want for himself.

My mother bore her burdens by adopting a philosophy of strength through silence and perseverance. All marriages are difficult. Things were getting better. Her child would need a father.

At church, Mike was asked to be a Seventy—a high-ranking title amongst Mormons, an honor rarely offered to anyone who wasn't decades older than my father. The other members of the church saw it as a sign that he was very spiritual and destined for greatness. My mother was confused by the calling, but was proud and it offered a newfound hope. Mike adapted to being with the older crowd without difficulty. The older couples made my mother uncomfortable.

One night after work, my mother, now eight-and-a-half months pregnant, met Mike and the majority of his family to see a movie. Someone there caught Mike's eye and, as my mother explains it, by whatever secret sign they agreed to meet after the show. Mike and my mother had parked in opposite directions. In the dark, Mom started off to her car alone. Mike made his escape. Upon returning home, Mom found Gloria waiting for her. She had seen Mom walking alone and was furious with her son. She sent my mother to bed and waited up for him. When he returned, she lectured him on appearances. Didn't he know what it looked like he was doing?

Gloria's concern would soon be diverted. Worried that my mother would be unable to deliver due to her small stature, Gloria pressured the doctor to induce labor early. The doctor was sure that I would be born soon anyway and agreed. The nurses disapproved, but were overruled and they prepped my mother for delivery.

All the fetal monitors were in use, so my mother was told to wait. She was left unattended for hours until the doctor returned at noon and hooked up a fetal monitor. He broke her water and said it would be hours before I was born. He and Mike went to lunch. No one came to check on my mother until Mike returned an hour and a half later.

Mom complained of discomfort and told him that she thought I was going to be born soon. A nurse in the hall overheard and came into the room. She had assumed the room was empty. Checking the monitor, she saw that I was in grave distress. Rushing to the hall, the nurse demanded help. My mother's doctor came running, his assistant began scrubbing for delivery. It was too late for a c-section, so they cut my mother as far as they could. I wouldn't come. A nurse pushed on me, practically jumping on my mother as the doctor pulled. I was coming out face down, but there was no time to think on it. At last, I was pulled free.

June 9, 1976, just after 2 p.m. I took the stage, blinded by the light.

BY ANY OTHER NAME

They named me Ryan Michael. Why I wasn't named Jason isn't clear. Mike had been emphatic before the pregnancy, but had long since abandoned the name altogether. My mother wanted to name me Mark, but my father's sister had already taken the name for her son. He settled on Ryan. It was never discussed, but Mom believes it was because he thought someone they both knew named Ryan was gay. Maybe I just wasn't the son he had envisioned.

Weighing in at five pounds, ten ounces, I was the only baby in the hospital less than six pounds and I had a nursery all to myself. My father was thrilled and bought an outfit for me to wear home from the hospital. He didn't return until a few days later, when it was time to bring my mother and me home. I had been born on a sunny day but went home in the rain.

Returning to the condo with his wife and newborn son, Mike promptly exited. He needed to leave on a business trip to Colorado and would be gone the entire week. Gloria stopped in a few times during his absence, but for the most part, it was just Mom who was left to contend with me. I had my days and nights mixed up and as a result, she lived in a tired blur. By Sunday, she was happy to have my father return. The sleepless isolation had started to get inside of her.

For the first few weeks, I was a docile "bag of beans" during the day. Come evening, I had colic and proved to possess a considerable endurance as I screamed myself red for hours. Mom held me throughout many evenings, rocking and walking to comfort me.

When it came time for her to return to work, she found it difficult to leave me. I was delicate, precious. In the mornings, she'd leave and Dad would get me up and drop me off at Aunt Jackie's. Mom would spend her day rocking back and forth as she went about her tasks, her mind always wandering back to me. After work, she'd find me asleep on Jackie's bed. She'd tidy me up and bundle herself around me. Once home, she'd feed me a bottle and then try to fix dinner before my crying began. After eating, she would give me a bath and try to calm me so that I would be able to eat. On a good night, the milk would stay down. Most nights it didn't and the walking and the rocking ritual would begin.

Nearly two years into her marriage, my mother found love; she found it in me.

TROPES AND PERSONAS

That summer, my father took us to his company party where we were proudly displayed. One of his co-workers fussed over me and commented to my mother that it must have been wonderful to have Mike home the first week after I was born. Mom could only smile and play her part.

My father cherished his time with me as the most loving of fathers could, but I failed to give him the lasting peace that he had expected or my mother had hoped for. Mom was consumed by insecurity, self-doubt, and reasonless guilt. Maybe I sensed it in the way she clung to me; she thinks I did and that these feelings contributed to my inability to sleep through the night. Her doctor had encouraged her to start nursing me, but Mike did everything he could to prevent it. He wanted to be both my mother and father and would feed me from a bottle whenever he could. To please him, Mom gave up on nursing me, which only made my vomiting worse. She tried soymilk, which seemed to go down better, until I was able to go on to regular milk.

We'd see a lot of Dad's family. There would be parties on holidays and we would drop in nearly every Sunday. The Painter family was always kind to my mother, but Grandma Gloria was critical of her mothering skills and often suggested that she needed to be stricter with me. One evening, I was left with Gloria, who was determined to get me on a four-hours-between-feedings schedule by the time Mom came for me the next morning. Upon returning, Mike's sister Sherry told her I had cried almost the entire time I was there. Mom was upset, but thought better of saying anything about it to Gloria.

In those early days, I lacked a distinct personality. I was either quiet and still or flushed and frantic. Mom looked forward to doctor appointments for any insight and comfort. The doctor gave his best advice, but ultimately we'd just have to fight my way through it. As I grew older, I became a happy child, if a little on the shy side. I was always latching onto my mother, twirling her hair around my fingers to keep her close.

From the outside, our lives appeared ideal. My parents had college degrees, good jobs and a new condo, were active at church and in the community, and I was such a delightful little boy. Women would often approach my mother, stare dotingly at me and tell her how jealous they were of her life. My father liked the illusion and found comfort in always having someone to take to family gatherings and to sit with at church. It dwindled speculation, calmed his demons, and made him a part of the world, rather than opposed to it. But, even for him, the illusion only brought misery.

Frustrated and unable to find direction, Mom visited her bishop and tried to repent of any sin she might have committed. Her bishop told her to go home and be happy.

Home was not a happy place to be. Outside there was the charade, but behind the curtain there were only actors that—having been removed from the context of their performance—had no relationship. Mike had his secret places where he could find solace. Mom had isolation and a child full of screams.

As an apparent act of compassion, Mike took to the idea of finding Mom friends. Whenever he met gay men who were married, and often Mormon, he invited them and their wives to our home to meet my mother. He was always bewildered why she never took to the friends he was offering her. Mom found them to be vulgar and uncouth or docile and subservient women that she wanted no connection with. I suppose he was trying to show her that she wasn't alone, but pity makes for a poor foundation on which to build a friendship.

One afternoon, Mom received a call from a woman thanking her and Mike for being so supportive of her teenage son. Mike had bought him clothes and things he needed for school. She said how glad she was that Mike had taken an interest in him because he had no father. Mom was terrified by the implications. When confronted, Mike insisted that he just saw this kid working at a fast food restaurant and wanted to help him out.

In October, Mom's sister Terri married. We traveled to Wyoming for the reception. I consented to behave and spent most of the day asleep on a bed.

In December, I celebrated my sixth month and was lavishly spoiled by my father for Christmas. Mom's sister Cristi was married right after the holiday and once again, we went as a family to Wyoming for the reception.

HEATHER CIRCLE

I had taken over the den, displacing my father's finely tuned and organized wardrobe. It was time to buy a house. Designing his dream home was a project Dad could throw himself into. He started making plans and took his ideas to a draftsman. He looked for a builder; the bids came back very high. He turned to David, Jackie's husband, who had two uncles with a building business. They had been constructing smaller homes on the west side of the valley and were anxious to break into a new market. Their bid was much lower than the others. They were hired.

Dad picked out a $19,000 lot; they thought he was crazy. They were accustomed to lots costing up to, but never above, $5,000. No lot was worth $19,000. It was an undeveloped area and although the plans were in place for other houses to come in the next year, they would be the first to start building. The developer promised to have the amenities functioning by the time the house was finished. Building went ahead and was to be completed in May.

My father was involved with every minute detail. The builders put up with the constant meddling more because of their relationship with David than to satisfy Mike. Dad had always wanted a stained-glass window and paid an extravagant amount to a local artist; the window provided was poorly constructed and couldn't be used. He approached a different artist who made a less ornate window that they were able to install.

My mother's parents celebrated their twenty-fifth wedding anniversary, but Mike said we didn't have the money to attend and we remained at home while the rest of Mom's family gathered in Wyoming.

May came and the house was near completion, but the developer had yet to install any of the necessities. We had already promised Dad's grandmother, Nana, who had just sold her house, that she could move into our condo on June 1st. June came and the developer had done nothing. The house was completed but we weren't allowed to move in until the developer fulfilled his end. The most we could do was store our furniture and boxes in the garage.

Luckily, Jackie and David were moving out of their apartment and we were able to slide in just as Nana moved into the condo. Lynne, my father's sister, began to look after me on days when Mom worked. With his dream house sitting empty, my father started in on legal action against the developer. By July, nothing had changed except for extensive damage caused by the rats that swarmed the garage and ate their way through the boxes.

In August, a court ruled against the developer. He was required to pay for the damaged items and provide the improvements. October came and we were stilling living in the apartment. Work in the development continued but the contractors only got the water and sewer in before the weather turned against them. Mom busied herself by making me a clown costume for my first Halloween and started her tradition of dressing up the house for the holidays by creating her own decorations.

In November, we were given permission to move into the house. It still didn't have a paved road, sidewalk, or front porch. An extension cord temporarily provided power, but there was no stove, so we used a hotplate and a toaster to cook with. We didn't have a telephone. Sometimes, the extension cord would get unplugged and would leave the house without power. Fortunately, the cold weather kept the muddy road frozen solid and allowed our little red Volkswagen to pass in and out of the isolation. Mom was just thankful to be in a house and not out camping.

Due to the delays and difficulties, the builders lost money on the home and left the east side housing market, never to return.

My mother's parents came and stayed for Christmas. Three years into the marriage and on the surface, life was pushing forward. A new house, a baby boy, her parents and a Christmas tree with presents; it was like starting anew. Everyone played his or her part with precision and Christmas seemed a resounding success. Only Grandma Beverly saw the truth and pulled her daughter aside and asked if she ever thought Mike would ask for a divorce. Mom was shocked. No, not now that I was born.

Within two weeks, Mike moved out of the house.

FLOWERS AND GHOSTS

Whenever my mother and I visit my father's grave, we bring extra flowers for Nana who is buried with her husband on the other side of the cemetery. The only memory I have of her is more of an urban legend than an actual experience. After she died, mom rented the condo to a family that claimed whenever they brought home flowers, the ghost of Nana would torment them.

Even as a child, I liked a good ghost story, but it was made all the more credible considering Nana's last name was Flowers.

Unfortunately, that story isn't nearly as appealing as it once was. One of the revelations that came from talking with my father's siblings is the unhealthy relationship that Gloria had with Nana, her mother. Gloria's penchant for cruelty was a lesson she learned from her possibly-alcoholic mother.

Gloria became estranged from Nana for many years. It was my father who tried to reconcile the two.

WILDERNESS

The bishop invited them to come to the New Year's Eve party at church. Mike said that they would be there. Later at home, Mom asked if she could buy a new dress for the party. He said, "We aren't going. I told the bishop what he wanted to hear." Within days, Mike said he was going to leave for a while. He was confused and unhappy and was making her unhappy.

He left us to live with friends downtown. We still saw him quite often. On days that my mother worked, he would get up early and drive to our house. She would leave and he would ready for work, get me up and dressed, before taking me to his sister Lynne's house. Most weekends when my mother worked, he would look after me.

One afternoon, my mother was struck by an unlikely idea: Did Mike know what he was doing was wrong? It was naïve, but she believed that if he would only recognize the gravity of his choices, he would have an epiphany and their nightmare would be over.

Yes, he knew, but it wasn't entirely his fault. He was perfectly aware that his standing in the Church was in jeopardy, but no matter what they did to him, he was still going to be part of the Church.

Their bishop asked them to go to marriage counseling. He found them a nice, most likely Church-approved, counselor. Mom was apprehensive; she was afraid that everything had been her fault. Maybe she hadn't cleaned well enough, or cooked well enough, or been as outgoing as she needed to be. Maybe she wasn't attractive enough.

The counselor spoke to them together and then separately, before bringing my mother back. He thought there was little chance that the marriage would survive and that she should prepare for divorce. He told her miracles happen, but not to expect one. My dad was referred to a professional who dealt with "recovering homosexuals."

Over the next few months, Mike would claim that he was going to church and attending meetings with Affirmation, a newly formed support group for gay LDS members. He met often with the bishop and was always promising him that he would come back and go to counseling or whatever the bishop wanted to hear. The bishop would always come to my mother—optimistic for change. Mike would just say the bishop was a good man and he didn't want him to feel like he wasn't doing his job.

With my father gone, Mom was increasingly uneasy about living in an undeveloped neighborhood with no lighting. The uneven electricity caused blackouts and one evening, the smoke detector kept going off. Another night, a group of teenagers threw a party on the driveway just below her window. We still didn't have a telephone and had no way of contacting the police. She was vulnerable and afraid for the baby sleeping in the room next to hers. If I woke, would my cries scare the teens away or pique their interest?

Once after midnight, Mike came and climbed into bed with her. She remained awake for the rest of the night, wondering what was going on, but didn't want to scare him away by talking to him. When she got up for work, he told her he had been standing in line for basketball tickets and decided he'd get more sleep if he came out to the house.

Gloria contacted President Davey and he tried tirelessly to contact Mike. He finally had to wait outside of Mike's work to talk to him. Mike was upset; nothing changed.

In spring, the electrical and road improvements were finished and we had a telephone before the end of April. It provided a small sense of security where there had been none. Life was shaping into a routine again.

While dad's family was, for the most part, aware of the separation, my mother's was not. In May, her sister Terri asked if she could come and stay with us for a few days while her husband attended a funeral. Terri didn't want to travel with him because she was pregnant with only a few days before she was due to deliver. My mother agreed. Knowing it would be fairly obvious when Terri arrived, she told her Mike had moved out in January. Terri was shocked. Immediately, Terri called Jackie and their mother. Grandma Beverly had guessed that something was amiss, but Jackie hadn't suspected anything was going on.

My father put money down on a new condo; the house would need to be sold.

ONE MAN, MANY FACES

I like to imagine my father walking Castro Street with a confident stride, his hips swaying free. He's left his ill-at-ease self in Salt Lake International.

Traded it for the comfort of an anonymity that would evolve into friendships unburden by expectation. How far did Michael need to run away from home to find himself?

He couldn't be him, not where he was known and admired. So, my father went to great lengths to appear as the person that people wanted him to be. It must have been exhausting to live with pockets brimming with lies and excuses. Did he believe that his clumsy magician's tricks—a misdirection and sleight of hand—could distract from what was obvious? If you dared to look closely, you'd find the seams.

He had a rolodex for one world and a black book for the other. A double life is really just two half-lives, never intended to converge. What if the man behind the curtain was cheered when he stepped on to the stage? Allowed to fulfill his potential without the weight of speculations and self-doubt, who would he be?

UNTIL DECEMBER COMES

Mom found a development nearby where they were building twin homes. Our realtor suggested she go to a lender that had been set up by women for women, believing they would be most likely to approve her loan. Traditionally, a woman's employment wasn't even considered in the process. It had only been in the past few years that banks would even think of giving a woman a loan. Despite her steady income, she was told they wouldn't be able to help her. She approached a more traditional lender and was told they couldn't consider her application unless a divorce had been filed.

She had never wanted a divorce; it was unthinkable. Mike had always said he wouldn't file and that it would look much better for her if she were the one to do it. She had assumed they would be able to remain married and simply live apart. Our house sold and we would need to be out by August. Her hand was forced. With the help of her bishop, she found a lawyer. His expertise was Constitutional Law and he had never handled a divorce case, they assured him that it would be an easy and cooperative divorce. He met with my mother and father separately to fill out various forms to determine how possessions would be divided, child support, and visitation rights.

My father had agreed to a modest child support and was willing to divide all their belongings. Ownership of the condo where Nana was living was divided between Nana and my mother. Both would responsible to split the mortgage payments. My mother was shocked to find that my father's visitation rights with me were contingent on him having a temple recommend. She had to reread the document twice to confirm she had understood it properly. The papers were filed in June. They would go before a judge in three months.

With the divorce filed, we were able to get a loan for the house. Like before, we would be the first people to move into the development. This time, the basics were already available. All of the houses were based upon the same floor plan but we were able to request a few changes (wood flooring in the entry, bookshelves in the living room, etc.). When we went in to sign the paperwork, we learned someone had canceled the final inspection and we were told we would not be able to close on the house. The surprise was too much for Mom to bear. After her brief breakdown, they decided that we could move in and pay rent until they could get the final inspection done.

On the day we moved in, after everyone left, the foreman returned with a six-pack of beer, certain that my mother would want to express her gratitude for his efforts.

In September, my parents went before the Judge. The divorce would be final on Christmas Day. Not wanting to associate the holiday with her divorce, Mom asked that they change the date. The Judge made the divorce immediately final and banged his gavel. This wasn't exactly what my mother had in mind. The divorce would finalize on December 15th.

Though it had been discussed, our lawyer had forgotten to include child support in the paperwork, but my father paid it along with our portion of the condo payment we were to split with Nana. Mom got the practical things; he took the decorations except for the grandfather clock. It had been a present and she wanted to keep it. He bought us a new TV and visited us often. He said therapy was going well. What exactly this entailed, we don't know. It has been said that he tried shock therapy and that at least once, he was written up as "cured." He never wanted to stop the divorce proceedings, but always spoke of coming back to us.

December 14th came and Mike was at the door in the morning. He said he was cured and would be coming back. He asked Mom to call and stop the proceedings. She agreed, but only if he came home that day. He couldn't leave Kent at Christmastime; they had made so many plans. She refused to call the lawyer. He insisted he would be remarried before she was. The following day, my parents were divorced.

AVERSION

He said he was cured. I prefer to think that my father's claims to have gone through various forms of conversion therapy was a smoke and mirrors act. The idea of him suffering through any kind of "treatment"—be it psychological, physical, or chemical—is heart wrenching.

For some, it is important that my father was willing to go to great lengths to try and chase away his attraction to men. It serves as evidence that deep inside Mike was so committed to his faith that he'd endure whatever hocus pocus pseudoscience was thrown at him. The option of accepting and loving himself for his uniqueness wouldn't have been considered as an option. For them, the moment he stopped seeing himself as broken was the point where he was beyond help.

I don't know why father would try to resuscitate the marriage. I suppose that even as the Titanic sank, there were those who took up buckets against the whole of the sea.

If my father was truly determined to change, what could science do that his faith in God had not? Those promises were already broken. If he had believed, belief failed him.

THEN THERE WERE TWO

Divorce is supposed to change everything. In our case, the physical routine remained exactly the same. Psychologically, things did change as Mom took on a heavy amount of the blame for the divorce. Culturally speaking, good Mormon housewives weren't supposed to get divorced. There are no Sunday School lessons that tell young women how to handle a post-divorce life. She had been taught that a successful marriage was predicated upon getting married in the Temple. It sounded like a guaranteed promise but someone forgot to mention that free will of others could get in the way.

We were fortunate that my mother had gone to college and disregarded her counselor's advice to frivolously pick a major. My father wanted to believe that he would eventually make enough money so that she wouldn't have to work. He spoke of this even after the divorce. It was a lovely thought, but it wasn't practical.

Even before the divorce it was difficult to go to church without my father. I know she struggled, felt alienated, and couldn't shake the idea that she was standing in a spotlight. Maybe it was all in her head; that didn't make it any less real. One week at church, I was on the floor quietly playing with a toy car. Another little boy came over with his car and I loudly revved up my car's imaginary engine. A woman in the front row stood up and told my mother that if she couldn't keep me quiet then she should get me out of the room. Mom picked up the car and me and went home. Later that day, someone from church, the Relief Society President, came and explained that the woman was very sick with MS and often was unable to attend church. It kept Mom going to church but it didn't take the sting away.

Things were made all the more difficult when we moved into our new house. Mom would have to meet a new bishop and face another room full of strangers with a child at her hip and no husband by her side. Would she have to tell her story a thousand times? How much was she willing to tell?

If I hadn't been born, it would have been easier for her to blend back into Mormon culture. Mom has always looked younger than she is and could have easily passed as a beautiful young socialite without any baggage. She would have been embraced by women and sought after by men and no one would need to be wiser. As it was, I made all of that impossible.

EMAIL EXCERPT: AVENUE ADDENDUM (EVERYTHING SAID & DONE)

He told me that I should wait for someone who, like he and his wife had, had waited for their first kiss over the altar.

That stuck in my mind and when your father made a similar statement to me. I guess I took it as some kind of a sign and when he said that he was not attracted to me, it did not worry me like it should have. At times I have felt set up by the bishop's comment or maybe it was the Lord's way of setting things into motion. Maybe your dad needed to feel that the Lord had not forgotten him and still had faith in him or maybe he needed the chance to try or something else entirely.

I guess from my own perspective and to salve my own conscience I would like to think that it was not a mistake to marry your dad and bring you into this difficult situation but that it was all a part of the plan and we are playing the parts and the challenges that we chose and accepted in our pre-mortal lives. To think that it was a mistake and I dragged you along on this twisted path when you merited an easier road.

I guess I do not want this to appear that I was set up by the bishop to make a mistake.

I don't think that the Lord sets us to fail. Although He may give us trials to strip us down to what is really important. I think that He may have known that the marriage would not survive but I don't think that He considers it a failure just fulfilling His purposes. It just focused us differently.

FATHER & SON

There were many who thought that my father should play a limited role in my life. Some even wanted to use me as a way to punish him. Mom thought he suffered enough on his own. She knew I needed to have him in my life and she worried that as I grew older, cultural pressure might lead me to reject him. He loved me—there was no question in that. She worried about the world he would take me into. The prevailing belief was that most, if not all, gay men were pedophiles. Seeking professional advice, a family counselor told her that the statistics said I should be safe, but my father should never leave me alone with his friends.

My father's world was a mystery. Even after years of being married to him, Mom could only guess and speculate. His misguided attempts to incorporate her via the "Suffering Wives' Club" offered no real insight. I think she would have preferred to know less about his life than she did. She wanted to protect me from knowing more than I had to. She did what many would call unthinkable: she trusted him.

I'm told that when Mom worked, Dad would take care of me in the mornings and often leave the office early to pick me up from daycare and keep me until Mom gathered me on her way home. I wish I remembered these little details. Learning of their existence offers a little comfort that's tempered by guilt for forgetting them in the first place.

WINDOW SHOPPING

When my father first left us, Mom spent as little time at the house as possible; its emptiness was unbearable. This meant we would often go to the Cottonwood Mall. Locked into an umbrella stroller, we'd walk up and down the length of the complex. As long as she went fast enough, I was entertained and didn't effort my way out my seatbelt. If she wanted to stop and look at something, I would liberate myself from the stroller and run and hide in the nearest clothes rack. Typically, this actually allowed my mother the opportunity to look around for a few minutes before having to wrestle me from under the clothes and back into the stroller. The only problem was, I liked to sneak from one rack to another and on at least one occasion, my evasive maneuvers left Mom in a panic.

Like most children, I did my share of crying over items that would eventually be lost or tossed aside. Like most parents, my mother ended up filling a junk drawer with cowboys and war generals, marbles and jacks, and five-cent stickers to silence the tantrums.

When I grew too large for the stroller, the real circus act began. There was something about the gravity in stores that made my shoes shrink and my torso balloon with weight. Within fifteen minutes of entering a store, my legs throbbed and swelled under the pressure of my massive upper half and my feet begged for relief. Mom only had two options: carry me, or relent and just go home. One evening, my mother was certain a man was following us. As I dragged my complaining feet through the parking lot, fear unnerved her. Independence wasn't easy and vulnerability wasn't limited to houses in the middle of nowhere.

Mom learned her lesson and mostly went shopping when I was with my father. It made for a more pleasant experience for the both of us.

STILL, CLOSER

My father's condo was less than a mile away from our new house in Murray. Generally, this was a good thing because it made it easy for me to see my father. And, because of the sheer number of Mormons who lived in the area, my father was assigned to attend church in a different building. His close proximity did, however, come with some unexpected disadvantages. One day, Glen Maynes, our mailman and a counselor in our bishopric, stopped by on his daily route and asked my mom a few questions about my dad. Rumors were circulating and the truth was there to be seen, but no one wanted to see it. Glen and his wife, Norma, had known my father and his family years before. Mom got the impression that my father's bishop was planning on calling him, but we don't know if it ever happened. Later, they realigned the boundaries of our congregation and my father was put into ours. It was strange for my mother but he never attended. She would be asked about him from time to time. Most were innocent questions, some were more leading. My father said he was attending a singles ward elsewhere.

AIRPLANE ARTISTRY

If talent were based entirely on desire and practice, I would have been a child prodigy in crayon composition. I was particularly fond of motorized vehicles (which somewhat explains my love for riding on the vacuum as Mom cleaned) and metropolitan landscapes, which eventually evolved into space battles (blame *Star Wars*), and the occasional sketch of E.T. (blame Spielberg). I spent hours sitting under the window at my little wooden table. The TV provided clatter and distraction as I played god of creation. Mom would be in the kitchen or working outside in one of her gardens. Bored with paper, I decided to move onto a new medium. The walls had yet to gain any personality and could do with a few airplanes, I thought. Using red, I began. The designs were void of aerodynamics—just loops and lines that resembled winged whales drifting through the universe. Nevertheless, I was quite pleased with my abstract representations.

Mom bought brown wallpaper and covered up my masterpiece.

Truthfully, I don't remember drawing the airplanes; this is by no means a plea of innocence. Drawing airplanes on the walls is exactly the sort of thing that I would have done. I do remember hearing the story many times over the years. Maybe I should feel guilty; I can't help but be proud. Someday, someone is going to peel away the wallpaper and be amazed by my attention to detail.

A PROPER EDUCATION

I've never been very good at sleeping. In my earliest of years, the only proven method to get me to still my flailing arms and legs was to stick a bottle in my mouth. Even as I grew older, Mom was hesitant to take away my "magic sleeping pill." The last thing she wanted was to return to the ceaseless crying that dominated my infancy. By the time I was two years old, my dependency on the bottle lessened to the point where I only needed it when I settled into bed. This was socially unacceptable for Dad's sister Lynne. The problem was that my cousin Heath, Lynne's son, was my age and had given up on the bottle long ago. A combination of Lynne's pressure, my habit of biting through the plastic nipple and the ensuing flashflood made Mom decide it was time to move past the bottle.

I was furious. After a brief scuffle and an endless amount of tears and yelling (all of which came from me), she agreed to let me keep the bottle. There was a catch: I was down to my last nipple and she wasn't buying any more.

That night, I bit through the last nipple.

I remember sitting on the couch and staring at the wall. I was upset, but not with my mother. She had left it in my hands and I forced the conclusion. I don't know if I planned on that nipple lasting forever but I certainly thought it would last more than a night. I had no choice but to go cold turkey.

A few months later, when the world yet again frowned upon my lack of progress because I was still wearing a diaper, Mom was at a loss as to how to get me to change my routine. I was stubborn and accustomed to life as it was.

Following my third birthday, we made the routine visit to Dr. Thomas. He asked how my training was going. My mother was forced to admit the miserable truth. He looked at me and asked what it would take to get me potty trained. I said, "A Hungry, Hungry Hippo Game." We bought one on the way home and I was potty trained.

Granted, soon after, Mom would find me urinating all over the bathroom walls. Nonchalantly, I told her I was cleaning.

AFTER A FASHION II

By the time I was potty-trained, I had become obsessed with fashion. I'm not sure where it originated but I'll blame aggressive Saturday morning advertising. As always, fashion starts with underwear. It was the golden age of Underoos and any self-respecting superhero wouldn't be caught dead without a clean pair. It wasn't exactly something you could share with the world but among friends your collection was something to be flaunted. Next was the t-shirt. This may have been the most important element of the ensemble because it was the most visible. Did it have a "character" on it? I'm not talking about symbols, trademarks, or cheesy embroidery of the brand name. I mean: Goofy, Batman, G.I. Joe, Snoopy, Darth Vader, Superman, Mickey Mouse, or Big Bird. The Izod alligator was pushing it, but I'd let it pass. Plain shirt? Striped shirt? Stick Murky Dismal or a Care Bear on it and we'll talk. Pants? Well, pants are a problem. Shoes? They hadn't really tapped into that licensing goldmine yet. Pajamas? Yes! I would have gladly skipped the formalities of proper dress for a life spent in pajamas. Add a cape and I was practically flying. Throw in a table to jump off of and I actually flew!

The only thing better than pajamas was a proper costume but Mom only made those for special occasions.

THE TROUBLE WITH METHOD ACTORS

One Sunday, I went to church dressed in a sailor suit. A little girl approached and commented on my appearance. I quickly responded by saying, "I'm Popeye the sailor man, toot, toot!" Each toot was emphasized with a right and then a left punch. It was a traumatic experience for the young lady.

I'm going to blame film director Robert Altman for this incident. Mostly because I can't quite figure out where this moment fits on the timeline but I have wonderful, vivid memories of seeing his 1980 adaptation (starring Robin Williams and Shelly Duvall) in the theater as part of a double feature.

I'd like to think this was the only time I ever hit a girl, but I probably threw a couple uppercuts and jabs at my mother along the way.

PROPHETIC METAPHORS

When I was two or three years old, my mother bought a decorative ghost to hang on the front door for Halloween. It was flimsy, made of thin plastic, like a reversed mold, white with a wide smile, and black eyes full of magic. I could have called it Casper or something equally plain and stolen but I proclaimed its name to be Dream. Something resonated inside me. Was it in the eyes? Perhaps the smile as it stretched wide? Even in looking back, stretching for the smallest of details, I smile at the memory.

One morning, pulling out of the driveway, I noticed that Dream was missing. My mother and I, probably without even having me demand it, drove around the neighborhood searching for my precious friend and finally found him blown up against a fence. She retrieved him and repositioned him on the front door.

Days later, the ghost would disappear again. We searched for hours but my Dream remained elusive, never found. I spoke often of my missing Dream with my mother, trying to come to terms with the loss. I never believed the wind had taken it; it had been stolen or Dream had wandered away by choice to be with someone more deserving. Still, it had been found once, could it be found again?

I never doubted my Dream's return. For years, I've waited patiently and not-so-patiently for that shapeless "it" to reappear.

LOVE BITES AND BRUISES

After their divorce, the relationship between my parents vastly improved. My father confided in my mother, offering a view into his life that wasn't always easy to look at. A number of his relationships were physically abusive.

A decade ago, when I first learned about the abuse, it broke my heart. My father was a passive, tender soul who cried the one and only time that he spanked me. I don't remember what I had done but I do remember deciding that I would never do anything to warrant a spanking again.

The more recent revelations about the sour, vituperative atmosphere of my father's childhood adds a new dimension to these details.

I've always worried that my father felt like he deserved to be treated poorly because he had been told that being gay made him a pariah before God and family. He may have made peace with religion, or quietly abandoned it, but the constant verbal reminders that he was lesser would have inevitably impacted the way he saw himself.

The more frightening thought is that he was accustomed to it. That it had nothing to do with the way he viewed himself—it stemmed from how he was raised. He knew that the abuse was wrong, but was ill prepared to avoid it.

NEWS OF THE WORLD

I've spent the majority of my life learning how little I know. The more I live, the more humbled I become. I have seen greatness in the painter's stroke, devastating realism captured in performance, extraordinary kindness from a mother, and brilliance in a jazz pianist's hands. For all the experience in the world, I'm still the little boy sitting at the undersized wooden table, watching the morning news while eating breakfast. It's early, 5:30 I think, long before dawn and soon I'll be sitting in my mother's car as we drive to wherever and whoever is taking care of me while she works. I would have preferred an episode of *He-Man* or *G.I. Joe* but apparently me and the five other kids who were awake at that early hour didn't make up a powerful demographic. So, the morning news it was.

This might seem insignificant—waking up to watch the news while the rest of the children of the world slept—but I've considered it to be one of the defining elements of my introduction to the world and how it related to me.

Looking back, I'm surprised I grasped as much as I did. The Cold War was wrapping up, although no one could have predicted that. Hours upon hours were devoted to President Reagan's "Star Wars" program. All those primitive, computer-generated graphics with white missiles firing from remote areas of Russia to heavily populated cities in America (sometimes riding on the back of a red, arching arrow). Depending upon the tone of the report these missiles (and arrows) would either be destroyed by another set of missiles coming from the opposite direction or sneak through the defensive barrier and land in Middle America (insert little explosion graphic here). It was either a brilliant idea that would ensure Americans were untouchable, even when it came to nuclear war, or the biggest waste of money the world would ever see. From the news perspective, I don't think they cared either way as long as it continued to capture their audience's attention. Was I sucked into the craze? I don't know. I was smart enough to know that this "Star Wars" program had absolutely nothing to do with the films. I didn't confuse the U.S.S.R. with the Galactic Empire; maybe I was supposed to. I blindly had faith in President Reagan; my mother seemed fine with him and that was enough to pacify me. I had no concept of real politics and had no interest in it. As far as the effect of this "cold" war? I felt none of it. I had no sense of the historic tensions between countries. The only wars I was overly concerned about were those I fought in the flowerbeds.

Thankfully, the news wasn't all angled to generate paranoia. There were always the farm reports to remind me of exactly how mundane everyday could be. I still have the images of cows chewing and large machinery spilling out grain burnt into my mind. There was also the "strength of the dollar" bit where they'd show all the little country flags. The common thread from one story to the next was always money.

One particular morning, they reported that someone had spent millions of dollars to purchase a painting of some sunflowers in a vase by someone named Van Gogh. What a waste, millions of dollars for a painting that you won't even hang on your wall! I knew of some airplanes behind the wallpaper that were twice as interesting as sunflowers in a vase. I'd draw some more for a dollar, a notebook full for ten.

AIDED BY THE PAST

It is here that my mother began to keep a journal. It greatly aided the timeline but there are many events that are not referenced in her writings and exist in a blurry area. I will do my best to place them properly. However, in searching for truth, I have found it is best to consider the sum, not the order of the equation.

JANUARY 11, 1980

I was very impressed upon to begin a journal two years ago this month, but at the time I was entering a period I thought I would like to forget and never reflect back on. But now I know although it has been a great trial I have experienced more growth and personal satisfaction than ever before. I no longer wish to blot out this segment of my life, but to share it.

I will begin by telling a little bit about myself; I am twenty-seven years old, I am almost five feet tall and weigh about 97 pounds (which includes over two pounds of Christmas goodies). I have short, curly, dark brown hair. I work as a medical technologist at LDS hospital. I have worked there 5 ½ years. I live in Murray, Utah with my son Ryan who is 3 ½ years old. I have been divorced for one year and separated for a year previous to that. I hold three positions in the Ward (South Cottonwood 1st); I am a visiting teacher, I teach the four year olds in Junior Sunday School every other week and I am the homemaking leader in the Single Parent Relief Society. I sometimes feel guilty because I have such fun and rewarding jobs.

My goals for this year include starting this journal, writing bi-monthly and when I have something special to write; finishing the Book of Mormon by April Conference; attending the Temple monthly; and of course moving closer to marriage.

COMPASSIONATE SERVICE

Mom was unusual in a few ways and this made her very useful. She was a single parent, which at the time was a tightrope walk for the LDS Church, but more importantly, she was independent and still active in attending church. Her role was fairly simple, in that she was asked to befriend single mothers, particularly those who felt ostracized, and check on them to make sure they were surviving. I'd often go along as she did her visiting. I don't remember any preaching, just the dropping off of treats or sitting in unfamiliar living rooms, minding my own business while Mom talked with other women. Mom says I was very patient. I thought that's what all kids and their mothers did.

FEBRUARY 5, 1980

Today I am home for a while alone. Ryan is starting in a daycare center and he is getting used to it in small doses. He has his first full day tomorrow. For the last 2 ½ years his aunt Lynne (Mike's sister) Meadows has taken care of Ryan and done a good job. But the time has come to make some changes and this is one of them.

CHANGE

I only have happy memories of my time spent at Lynne's. She had older children, which was different from going to my aunt Jackie's. My cousin Heath, who was the same age as me, was somewhere in the middle of the sibling hierarchy and by extension, so was I. I remember many card games, particularly Go Fish, and watching television. We raced cars through a track that was lined with rows of tiny plastic sacrament cups (every Sunday I tried to keep my cup to add to the collection, but was never able to sneak it past my mother). And I remember that Brett, who was at least four years older than me and grew too tall to fit in his bed, had a nice collection of *Star Wars* toys that he'd bring out every so often to tempt me and Heath with.

Following the divorce, Tim, Lynne's husband, would often stop in to make sure we were doing well. As these visits became more and more frequent, my father pointed out to Mom that Tim would always park down the street away from our house as if his kindness, or the motivation behind it, came with a sense of guilt. After Tim's next visit, Mom was saddened as she watched him walk down the block to his car. Mom tried to discourage him from coming alone; it was clear that it would be best if he didn't come at all.

FEBRUARY 5, 1980 CONTINUED

This past month I received a telephone call from [Nana], Mike's Grandmother and a visit from his mother: both asking me to consider re-marrying Mike. I could never do it unless it was what the Lord required of me and He gave me a lot of support. But the Lord has blessed me with knowledge and told me many times that this is not what He requires of me. It upset my father a great deal that they will not let me alone to find some peace.

DAYCARE

Murray Day School was my first public daycare. It wasn't bad, and if you took out the tomato juice, I'd call it relatively painless. Mom hated leaving me. I was always one of the first children to arrive and there was little to distract me. Usually, she left me in front of a TV, hoping that would enter-tain me. Compared to going to Jackie's or Lynne's, there certainly was an adjustment period. The other kids weren't your cousins so they felt no obliga-tion to befriend you. The friends you did make were because of circumstance and lacked the bond felt between more traditional friends. The adults weren't family either; they were interested because they were paid to be. Even as a child, I knew the difference. Most of all, there were so many kids that you could even lose your sense of self in the shuffle.

Mom was still working two or four days, depending on the week. The day-care suggested that it would be better for me if I came every day and made it a routine, rather than just bringing me on the days she worked. It wouldn't have cost her any more; she had to pay for those days anyway. She decided she'd rather have me at home.

I'm forever thankful.

JEFF

I think that we both have great and bittersweet memories of Jeff. If you had a challenging childhood it did not come close to his. He was always a tattered rag-a-muffin. But so loveable and cute—he just pulled on your heartstrings. I wish I could have adopted him and you would have had a brother. His mother was so typical of my single parents. Her only hope to survive was to find someone to rescue her. Paul was not a shining knight—not for her and especially not for Jeff. Jeff was such a good friend to you and loved to be at our house. I remember picking you up from school one early fall afternoon and driving to Park City to see the leaves. I re-member the Star Wars on our front steps and in the flower gardens. His hair was always long and hanging in his eyes and his face was always smudged. He always looked so hopeful.

Jeff is a rather abstract thing to me now, so far removed and yet so much a part of me. I think of him often these days, particularly when the world turns against me. I hope that somewhere he's smiling, two teeth missing, eyes full of warmth and a sense of happy recklessness bubbling beneath their surface. We were two of a kind—lonely, drawn together and nothing else mattered.

Despite my situation, I never knew of brutality. My mother had prepared herself, ensured our future with her education. Jeff's world was laced with a struggle that suggested defeat long before it offered opportunity. Of course, I was too young and distracted by innocence and misunderstanding of how the world worked to see anything more than the little boy who made afternoons slip away into evenings. When I look back through older, clearer eyes, I see the poverty and pain that became Jeff's world the moment that he stepped away from our yard. I can't help but wonder if he ever made it out alive.

He would come over, it seemed like he was always next to me playing *Star Wars* in the planter boxes or *He-Man* in the unfinished basement. He only had a few toys of his own but I never minded sharing mine with him. More than anything, I was just happy to have someone around. It was a glorious time. We were fueled by imagination. You could call it an escape; I call it the luxury of childhood. Don't like your world? Dream up a new one. In these new landscapes, fragile as they were, two silly boys became heroes as we saved the galaxy an infinite number of times from evil.

We became friends because my mother knew his mother as one of the many single women that she was asked to visit. Mom knew I wanted a friend and she saw that Jeff needed somewhere safe to run to. I never wondered why Mom was never quick to send him away, often stretching our days into the early evening. She'd offer lunch, dinner, a late snack and Jeff certainly didn't mind. I always considered it for my benefit.

There has always been the suggestion of physical abuse when I think of Jeff. How could a child tell the difference between a bruise and the dirt smeared thin across his arm after a day of intense flowerbed combat?

When school came along and dominated most of my time, Jeff, who was a year younger than me, started to slide out of the picture. Then Jeff moved; it was a relatively short distance but in a child's world anything beyond a block is an impassable distance. I missed my friend and wondered if he missed me. Mom seemed just as concerned for him. We'd both found someone special in Jeff and loved him. I wish he could have been my brother forever.

FEBRUARY 22, 1980

Last night I attended our Stake's Visiting Teacher's Conference. The speaker for the meeting was Brother Blaine Yorgansen. He gave an excellent talk on insecurity causing envy and jealousy. He stated that we can't do everything just as well as everyone else and we needn't feel insecure because we can't. We should live by the spirit and act when prompted and quit striving to be the "perfect" wife who can do everything.

This last week my two sisters (Jackie and Terri), their husbands (David and Mike) and their children (Jeremy, Brandon and Scott) came for family home evening. We talked to our sister Peggi who is a freshman at BYU and she told us that she and her boyfriend (Steve) are getting married about August 14. I am really very happy for them and told her so. She seems so young and yet at eighteen I also had the greatest love of my life and she is so much more mature than I was at her age. It was just a month ago I told a good friend of mine that I didn't worry much about a younger sister beating me to the altar.

Ryan is really enjoying his nursery school—finally—and it's especially nice not to have to rely on his father so much.

MY MAGICAL MOTHER

I remember being sick; I must have been four or five years old. In my head, I can only see the bathroom stall, metallic grey and my head's spinning. I was at daycare and too shy, stubborn, or afraid to tell anyone how sick I felt. All I wanted was my mother but didn't want to pull her away from her job; not because I thought I was less important, but because I didn't want to burden her. And yet, there she was, far earlier than expected, picking me up and whisking me away to home.

When I asked her how she knew I wasn't feeling well and needed to be picked up early, she said, "I just knew." This confirmed what I already knew: my mother was a Jedi able to sense disturbances in the Force. Maybe that made me a Jedi as well.

ENTERING EDEN

Looking back, there are numerous memories of days spent with my father that don't make much sense. For instance, I remember there was a small building on the grounds of my father's complex that was half a home and half a greenhouse. Where the living quarters ended and the garden began wasn't entirely clear. It is as if the living room fed into a kitchen that transitioned into a bedroom of roses. There was an open sack of soil, a bucket of fertilizer, and a hand shovel lying on the ground next to the refrigerator. You started in darkness and slowly moved south towards the brightness of the glass-bound garden. The aroma of the roses and soil was intoxicating.

The man who lived there was out of town and my father and I were simply checking up on the flowers. Maybe there was a cat that lingered in the shadows, a hidden king sleeping lazily on his carpeted throne. Dad explained that the man was a friend. This made perfect sense, even if roses weren't my father's favorite flowers.

I could return to where the building was and, assuming it still exists, untangle this strange memory of the garden house. I could, but I won't. My whole life, I have fought fiercely to retain as much of the innocence, hungry imagination and sense of wonder that defined me as a child. To know the truth behind every memory would sever my connection to the magical world of my youth. This memory will be allowed to retain its nonsensical existence.

MARCH 21, 1980

Ryan broke out with the chicken pox two weeks ago. He had a very light case, but we spent a week home alone together. We played games, read lots of stories and drew a lot of pictures. He was never at a loss for things to do; his imagination was running overtime. We made "the dish that ran way with the spoon" out of a plastic spoon and a paper plate and pipe cleaners; we played Little Red Riding Hood; we painted breadboards for gifts; he taught me school and wrapped up his matchbox cars and put them under a plant decorated as a Christmas tree. One morning he came and asked for a piece of bread, a few minutes later he was back for a glass of water, a few minutes after that he was back "passing the Sacrament" with his left hand tucked behind his back like Tony (the deacon across the street) does.

I just got back from a neighborhood "party." We have a new neighbor, Carman, who recently moved into our area. They had a little open house at Rick and Jill Steeds' to get to know her. She is divorced and so they especially wanted me to go and meet her as they are hoping to teach her the gospel and I could help by fellowshipping her and getting her out to the single parent activities.

The Elder's Quorum President from the Single's Ward was asked to go too, a mutual friend suggested we go together so he called and we did. He is very nice but I scared him away too. I don't know why I have such great luck. I asked him in (at 9:30) after we left the party but he went home to work on his home teaching districts. Am I that bad? I'm just a little depressed; I don't know what's wrong with me.

MY MOTHER, THE BEARER OF GIFTS

There was plotting, preparation, escape routes, and alternate paths should things go awry. Never go at the same time, do not allow them to establish a pattern. When in doubt, do something absurd, a bit corny or tacky, but by no means vulgar. Never be seen, leave no trace, and smile all the way home, knowing someone was standing on their porch scanning the bushes for evidence they'd never find. My role in this conspiracy was simple: run from the car, deposit the package, ring the doorbell, and be back to the car, which was usually parked around the corner or just far enough up the street to allow for a proper escape. Not an easy task for someone with such short legs and a chest full of throbbing heart. It was exhilarating¬¬, even if I complained by wanting a task far less secretive. Perhaps I could drive the car?

We could have been brilliant criminals. The world would have fallen in love with the dangerous duo of single mother and her child as we blazed a trail of robbery and mayhem across America. Some would have called us heroes—a rejuvenation of the French Revolution, American-style. Bonnie and Clyde would have nothing on us. Instead, we were kind neighbors. What a waste of panache and moxie.

This was the Twelve Days of Christmas, St. Patrick's Day, Easter, May Day, Fourth of July, Halloween, Thanksgiving, and whatever holiday my mother could make up as an excuse to treat those she loved, neighbors and the occasional stranger.

On more mundane days, she'd stroll up and ring the doorbell; I'd stand at her side, these things were always done in twos, waiting nervously for the door to open so that my mother could hand over a plate of cupcakes, cookies, or some other treat. In these instances, my role was to look cute; I preferred the mad dash for the car.

MAY 2, 1980

Last week my parents and my sister Peggi came down to Salt Lake (they live in Casper, Wyoming). My parents came to participate in a temple excursion. Peggi came down to look for a wedding dress and look for a job in Provo for next fall (at BYU). Ryan and I took her down to the campus. Ryan got a BYU T-shirt with Snoopy on it.

The whole family here in Salt Lake got together for a picnic at Murray Park.

Kathy Hogan, who lives across the street from me, called last week. She and Dan are getting a divorce and she wasn't doing too well. I've suspected something was going on but didn't exactly know. I took her to the Relief Society activity that night. I saw her in Church on Sunday and walked home with her. We had a couple good conversations. Last night after Ryan and I delivered May Day Baskets (26) the Bishop (Calvin Gilles) called and told me she was having a bad night. I called her and she came over and talked until 11. I can't really give her the answer to her problems but I can listen and help her think things out. I wish I could do more. Talking to her does make me realize how far I've come and that maybe there is hope in sight.

At times my life is so frustrating or maybe I'm just impatient.

I am going to the temple tomorrow at 6 a.m. with my ward—I can't think of a place I enjoy being more.

DINNER WITH MY GODMOTHER

When Carrie Fisher died, I took it particularly hard. I had been a *Star Wars* fan for as long as I could remember and had come to utterly adore Fisher's affinity with glitter, strength, and candor in the ensuing years. She lived the sort of life that made you believe that if she didn't die young, what could possibly kill her?

There was a personal connection in that my mother's best friend, Kathy, was my Princess Leia—beautiful and fiery with the kindest of hearts, a wildflower in a garden filled with domesticated creatures. Somewhere along the way, the fictional stories became interwoven with the real person. It was as if Leia was Kathy's alter ego.

The thought of losing her, my second mother who loved me as her own, was devastating. Yes, death became real to me when I was seven years old, but it still surprises and staggers me when someone dies. Kathy had known my father before my parents married. Like the passing of Grandma Gloria and Grandpa Bob, what stories would Kathy take with her?

Kathy also lived in the Avenues and attended the same church as my mother and father. She knew my father to be a very kind, loving person. Kathy recalls their bishop as a man who was obsessed with getting his congregation of single adults married—regardless of the cost. He had a poster that hung in his office that recorded the running total of marriages that had been brokered under his watch.

My mother would tell you that the bishop was a good man ill-equipped to face the challenge before him. I'm not sure that I would be so kind. He believed that marriage could "cure" any man of his "homosexual tendencies." It was his advice, to my father, which led to the marriage and divorce of my parents.

From a comfortable distance, his advice and beliefs seem archaic, ill-informed, and cruel. But popular opinion both in and out of Mormon circles at the time was—and sadly often still is—that being attracted to the same sex is a choice. Not being gay is as simple as not drinking coffee or abstaining from cigarettes. If you loved God you could easily give up the addiction. So, any "good Mormon" couldn't possibly be gay on a permanent basis.

Kathy, who had moved from the ward before my mother and father began dating, insists that had she known of the engagement, she would have not allowed the marriage to happen. As it is, she was gone and whatever role she could have played was not offered to her.

Kathy reappeared when her husband Dan built the neighborhood of duplex homes that my mother and I would move into. Kathy and Dan lived across the street from us.

Kathy insists that Mom did everything she could to avoid her. Mom disagrees, categorically denying that she'd run inside the house whenever she saw Kathy come out of hers.

I don't know that Mom would purposefully avoid Kathy, but would you blame her if she did? Being divorced was a dark mark in Mormon culture. My father's sexuality, which Kathy may have known, would have made things all the more complicated. The last thing my mother would have wanted was someone around who had a direct connection to the part of her life that she was trying to put behind her.

Kathy says when her marriage to Dan collapsed, it was the bishop who called my mother and asked her to check on Kathy, unaware that the two of them knew each other from years before.

Mom, who had watched Kathy scrape Dan's name off her mailbox, crossed the street and knocked on the door. In that moment, Mom found her best friend and our lives were forever benefited thereafter.

MY MISSING BROTHER

Mom was going to adopt a Native American boy to be my brother. Why else would I have a bunk bed? It sounds absurd. I thought it was a fact, until I started to explore my mother's perspective on my childhood memories. She had no idea what I was talking about.

Maybe it was a dream or something I saw on TV. Either way, it forced me to reconsider the past and explore where this misconstrued myth could have originated.

I found something buried away.

As a child, I had another theory about the empty bed. I obsessed over the idea that I had a brother who had died. At first, I thought he would have to be older than me, but as the story grew, it became clear that he would have been my twin. I wrestled with the idea of being alive while my other half lay secret in a cemetery somewhere. I spent many nights wondering if he had lived and I was the one to die, would he have been a better son?

In my early teens, a book of genealogy was published that included the Painter family. In its pages, it listed that I had a brother who had died. They also listed my father as still being alive.

MAY 15, 1980

Ryan is at his father's tonight so I have a few minutes to myself. I did go to the Temple with my ward and was really glad that I did. We had breakfast served by the Seventies at the ward house after the session.

The next morning we had a very good lesson in the Relief Society on living by the Spirit. During testimony bearing I was very moved to bear mine and did. I feel like I'm still working for acceptance. The more they get to know me the better I feel.

Last Sunday, Mother's Day, Ryan gave me some petunias and geraniums for the yard, also some garden shears. This week my neighbors put a fence up for me (I paid for the materials but it was a very appreciated effort). It is nice to have some privacy.

STILLNESS OF LIFE

Friday night at my father's was often spent drawing while my father watched *Dallas* (of which I remember absolutely nothing). In later years, Bryan, the only boyfriend my father deemed worthy of invading our time together, was also there. Come Saturday morning, Dad would wake me so that I could watch the *Smurfs* and then he'd promptly go back to bed for an hour or so. On one occasion in his groggy morning state, he accidentally turned the television over to the static of channel three. I watched a white-and-black storm for the better part of an hour; I believed my father could do no wrong and Papa Smurf would show up at any moment.

My father's condo was a strange place, in that designer magazine sort of way. Dark leather chairs, a giant stuffed pheasant above a black rock natural gas fireplace, deep couch with coffee table. Adjacent was a large dining room table with a chandelier hanging above it. Even the tiny kitchen had its character provided by a stylized old-fashioned phone that hung on the wall. A large bed and dresser dominated his bedroom. We never spent any time in these rooms. Our lives were played out in the den, which had a modest couch, small television, and upright piano in later years. It had none of the showiness of the rest of the condo. It was a warm room, while the rest felt like a sanitized museum. With exception of Bryan, all guests were entertained in the other areas of the house. Not that there were many guests while I was there. He went out of his way to make sure there would be little distraction during the time we spent together. Yes, there were small adventures here and there, but in many ways, his actions seemed to betray the public persona he had. Time with me was absolutely as normal as possible. The rest was him caught in the confusion of life, tossed to one side or another by his conflicted interests. Quiet was what he really wanted, which he felt when I was there with him.

JULY 19, 1980

On the 3rd of June Brother Fred Donkin asked me to be the chairwoman of the Single Parents Relief Society program. I was very overwhelmed by the calling but of course I took it.

It has been discouraging and a lot of frustrating effort. I am becoming very grateful for small successes.

Ryan's birthday went well. We had my side of the family over early and Ryan's father's side over later. Mike was here the entire evening. Ryan and I made a Big Bird cake that really turned out cute. We decorated with balloons and streamers and a big poster of Big Bird.

POINT OF REFERENCE

I remember this birthday; the cake looked just like the professional one in the picture that came with the pan. They always did. Mom's ability to produce cakes and costumes that surpassed the quality of store-bought items is legendary to this day. The giant Big Bird poster came with feathers and a blindfold. It was obviously a variation on "pin the tail on the donkey" but I've forgotten the specifics. It wouldn't be too difficult to simply pin a feather on a bird. Maybe that's the point.

Mom's family was always very kind to my father. His presence at any event was never a distraction of any sort. Mom has wondered how everyone kept such good behavior. I've always told her that they were simply following her lead. It was more than that—they liked him.

At a family gathering for Father's Day in 2018, my uncles Mike and David independently pulled me aside to share their kind feelings and memories about my father. These were conversations that I would have never been bold enough to start. I thought that bringing up my father, whose lifestyle would have gone against their long-held religious beliefs, might have felt confrontational. These men had been surrogate fathers to me. I had no interest in locking horns with them.

I've come to realize that my father was the first gay person that many people knew. AIDS had a way of pushing people out of their closets. My father betrayed the stereotypes, contradicted the brimstone preachers, and offered a different point of view. This asked some to either confront the way they saw the gay community as a whole, consider him an exception to the rule, or ignore his sexual orientation altogether.

JULY 19, 1980 CONTINUED

For the 4th of July Ryan and I drove to Casper, Wyoming. We had a real good time. I needed to get away. For the 4th Mom, Dad, my sister Peggi and her fiancé Steve, Ryan and I carried our lunches on our backs and hiked about 2 miles in on Muddy Mountain, had our lunch and walked out. Ryan really enjoyed it. We found a deer skeleton and Ryan was very intrigued by it. I gathered a large garbage sack full of pinecones for future projects.

We have had 2 marriages in our Relief Society in the past month. So far we have had 5 marriages, all in the Temple.

Thursday Jackie and I got material for a quilt for Peggi. We got it cut out and sewed together Friday. We will quilt it this next week. Peggi is getting married August 12 in the Salt Lake Temple.

TO LOSE IS TO WIN

I was a particularly competitive little boy when it came to board games. There were Monopoly games that lasted days. I'm not sure if Mom enjoyed the games as much as I did. I think she did. For me, they were heaven: a trail of sugar dipped sweets, little plastic cars full of pink and blue pegs racing through green plastic mountains, bright red cherries spilling out of baskets, hippos devouring pearls, and at least a thousand chutes and ladders to slide and climb.

Kathy tells me there was a particularly rough night when she came over to cry on my mother's shoulder. I talked her into playing a board game with me. Kathy claims that I purposefully lost in an attempt to raise her spirits. It must have been a trick I had picked up from my mother; a little affirmation of love that she inscribed into me.

AUGUST 16, 1980

This past Tuesday, August 12th, my sister Peggi Jeen Young and Steven W. Hopkins were married and sealed in the Salt Lake Temple. Elder Harman Rector Jr., Steve's mission President, performed the ceremony. It was lovely. Afterwards we talked and there wasn't a one of us that weren't personally touched by something he said. He came out very strongly against divorce and homosexuality. He talked a lot on birth control and raising children. He really focused on the covenant they were making and its long-range the new ¡6effect. He said that every kiss in marriage should be in remembrance of the covenants of marriage as the sacrament is of baptism. After we left the sealing room one of the temple workers pulled us aside and remarked that it must have been a very special experience to spend an hour with Brother Rector. His wife, Connie, was there also; she is a lovely woman.

Wednesday morning at 6:30 Ryan, my maternal grandmother Sara Tueller Fisher and I left for Casper Wyoming for their reception Thursday. It rained Wednesday night and part of Thursday. Clouds threatened but our prayers were granted and it did not resume raining until after midnight and continued most of Friday. Our early birthday party for our dad had to be moved inside Friday night.

Grandmother, Ryan and I left early in the morning and arrived home about 3pm. It was good to talk to my grandmother. We really hadn't for years. She cannot understand why I am not married. I tried to explain that I'm just barely really adjusting and what a mess I would have been to be married besides… but….

SING ME TO SLEEP

My father bought me a silver boom box, the sort you'd see on a Beastie Boys record or in a hip-hop video from the early '80s. I'd record the audio portion of television programs so that I could listen to them later. Sometimes I'd tape a *He-Man* cartoon episode and attempt to recreate the events with my collection of toys. Jeff and I would also record our *Star Wars* and *He-Man* battles and listen to them. I'm not quite sure what the thrill was; perhaps hearing ourselves wage war with a wide array of sound effects was self-affirming evidence that we were in fact brilliant when it came to childhood impromptu. Truthfully, I don't think there was a point beyond the fact that we could record ourselves.

At night, I would fall asleep listening to majestic tales pulled from the Disney archives, *Star Wars*, or classic literature repurposed for a child's intellect. My rampant imagination took me to the beginning and the end of all places. Only after the exhaustion of adventure could I leap from consciousness into dreams. Beyond the ether, I'd become the hero who could shake off the haunting call of Maleficent—which terrified me—and save Aurora from her fate as the sleeping beauty.

I don't know if I picked up this routine through my experiences at daycare where they would play stories like *The Black Stallion* while we struggled to unwind in the darkness of naptime, or if this was a replacement for all the rubber nipples I had bitten through. Maybe I had already learned that silence is a lonely place to be. I think it is the latter because I still find comfort in the muffle of indistinguishable conversations, footsteps on creaking boards, or tires grinding against the loose gravel of the road outside as I fall asleep.

COMPULSION

I'm in the toy section of the discount department store Grand Central watching Dad flip through the dangling Star Wars action figures. He's trying to find every character featured on the cover of the Creature Cantina Action Playset.

It's likely 1980 and *Star Wars Episode V: The Empire Strikes* Back has just arrived in theaters. I'm turning four and I've agreed that the playset would be a fantastic birthday present, but only if it's complete. Otherwise, I've determined that a LEGO knock-off will be my preferred gift.

He digs through the entire recently-restocked endcap, eight or so pegs holding five or six figures apiece. I don't know if my demand is greed or an early sign of the obsessive collecting that would follow me into adulthood.

Unable to find all ten characters featured in the picture, we leave with the box of plastic bricks.

I frequently played with the building blocks, but would still come to regret my decision. Dad clearly wanted to buy me the cantina.

SEPTEMBER 27, 1980

Tonight I attended the woman's session at the tabernacle. The General Relief Society President spoke and then members of the general board, one of them being single, and [the prophet] President Kimball welcomed us in his "still small voice that pierces the heart," and then Brother Boyd K. Packer addressed us. The Meeting was about "Learn then teach." Brother Packer really stressed the importance of Relief Society and attendance. It was an enjoyable meeting with a lot of encouragement to single sisters.

This past month as I was renewing my temple recommend I also talked to my bishop about a cancellation of sealing. I got the papers and filled them out and wrote a letter to President Kimball about the divorce. I really tried to be fair. Mike also had to write a letter telling the reasons for the divorce and if he consented to a cancellation of sealing. He wrote his letter, really made me the villain in the relationship and said that we could all be a family again; he could not consent.

At first I was just angry; it seemed he was trying to ruin my chances for happiness. But after I talked to the bishop and received a special blessing (the first I've received in this divorce) I felt much better and I haven't worried about it since. The bishop also promised me the deepest desire of my heart and that I would be led to the steps to take to attain it. There is only one desire down there that I know of: That is to remarry.

THE EDGE OF TOMORROW

My father would have been taught that because he was gay, there would be no redemption for him in this life and that his best hope would be to be spiritually tied to my mother and me in the next.

In a Mormon wedding ceremony that takes place in an LDS Temple, the words "'til death do we part" do not exist. The belief is that the marriage is sealed forever, extending beyond the mortal life. Once made, this sort of bond is not easily broken. Not even in the case of divorce.

This would have been an incredible burden for my mother and, possibly, a last thread of hope for my father. He might have believed that we'd be a happy family someday, somehow, somewhere. He spoke of remarrying my mother at times to fend off his family, but the idea was imbued with the wistfulness of fairytales. Not on his part, but on mine. I never believed that

Mom, Dad, and I would ever be a conventional family in this world or the next.

I thought that in the afterlife, we would be together much in the same way while we were alive. Me, with little hands outstretched, bridging the divide between them. I was blind to whatever tensions existed between my parents. There was never an effort on either of their parts to disparage the other. I wasn't forced to choose; I was allowed to love.

I've tried to find a scenario where my father's refusal to cancel the sealing made perfect sense and caused neither of my parents an immense amount of pain.

There aren't any.

I imagine him receiving the news that Mom wanted a full and permanent separation. Furious, heartbroken, and backed into a corner, he lashes out at my mother because God feels too far out of reach. He had been taught that being gay was a damnable sickness, casting a shadow over everything good that he could find inside himself. This life was forfeit and without the sealing, the next life would be too.

With the safety net of his covenants replaced with the vastness of promises unwritten, would God, having lost His own son, allow my father to keep his?

IMPOSSIBLE PRINCESS

The summer of 1998, I ran away from home. Not just down the street or around the corner; I left the continent for the UK. Left to my own devices, I spent summer living on couches and in rented spare rooms. It's something of a blur, awash in afternoons spent digging through secondhand vinyl records, reading Harry Potter novels while on trains, and catching an exuberant number of concerts and theater productions.

At no point did it resemble a Henry Miller or Irvine Welsh novel, but there were hijinks aplenty.

One adventure that feels tied to this story—rather than a wider look at my coming of age—takes place over the course of two nights, July 29th and 30th, at Shepherd's Bush Empire, a multi-tiered concert venue in London that holds around two thousand people.

My taste in music is generally centered on alternative and independent British artists from the eighties or those who are inspired by that era. However, there are numerous exceptions to the rule. One of those being Kylie Minogue.

1998 was a strange in-between period in Kylie's career. Her new album, *Impossible Princess* (initially released as a self-titled album due to the recent death of Diana, Princess of Wales), was warmly received in Australia, but was dismissed as inconsequential in the UK and Europe. Its North American release was canceled altogether.

As a result, Kylie performed only twenty-something shows in theaters, rather than arenas, in support of the album. Three in London, the rest were in Australia.

There was a Pride Festival atmosphere at the two shows I attended. Only, at that point in my life, I had never been to a Pride Festival. I was accustomed to being something of an outsider, but I had never been in a situation where, as someone who identifies as straight, I felt like the minority.

So, I didn't speak much, but I smiled every time they called me "darling." I thought about my father, how I loved him and wished that he could have been there to feel what I felt. Maybe he had, among friends, when the world wasn't looking or when he was with me and nothing else mattered.

In the twenty years since, I've only been able to see Kylie again a handful of times. Inevitably, by the end of her show I've sobbed, pulled myself together, and then cried some more. Dad always feels closer when Kylie is on the stage. She's our girl.

OCTOBER 22, 1980

My Relief Society job is really getting to my stomach. Right now I have a girl who is pregnant, one dating a married High Priest and one with a split personality (one of which is lesbian and really likes me). My stomach feels like someone has shot it full of holes. I have an appointment with a gastroenterologist on Friday. I'm really learning of President Kimball's counsel: Hate the sin, but not the sinner.

There is a little flicker of excitement in my life now. He probably doesn't realize it but he is. I have known John for about eight years. I went to school with him at BYU, then he came to Salt Lake City the same year I did, me to intern as a Med Tech at LDS Hospital and he to medical school at the University of Utah. He has been in Denver since just after I filed for divorce. I've written him a few letters this year and got a few back. The last month I've gotten a few humorous cards from him and they have really lifted my spirits. I've always felt like I knew him better than I do.

JOHN, THE CHARMING PRINCE

Charming was attractive, funny, a successful doctor, presumably straight, and for all intents and purposes, perfect. His letters meant everything to her. It was a safe way to ease back into feeling, using distance as buffer to disappointment. The smallest kindness gave her hope. Hope became expectation.

1981

JANUARY 4, 1981

The last year has been a good one. It has been 2 years since my divorce, so I've been alone for almost 3 years. I feel I am doing very well and Ryan seems to be doing well also. Everyone, his teachers, say he is very well-adjusted. This year my goals are much the same as last year: write in my journal, attend the temple at least monthly and, this year, resolving a relationship I have with John.

JANUARY 20, 1981

Today is a very important day in American history, we inaugurated our 40th president Ronald Reagan and the Iranians released the 52 hostages after 444 days of captivity. It has brought a renewed patriotic spirit to us all. If I hadn't been at work I would have gone out and bought a flag. Tonight Ryan and I watched the hostages deplane in Algeria and talked about the happenings of the day. They had talked about it at school. It surprised me what a 4-year-old can understand.

Peggi has announced she is pregnant.

THE BRIGHTEST LIGHT

There is a road that twists and turns through a forest where the trees touch the clouds and light glimmers through their leaves as if dancing through a string of glass baubles. My father is driving, telling me of a place in Montana that he owns, a place very much like this one and that someday we will see it together. There is a stillness, a calm in him that betrays all other memories I have of my father, outside of time spent in his den.

We would never see Montana, or anywhere quite as beautiful as this day in a forest I could not find again. Perhaps as I grew, the trees lost their height and the light ceased to dance. Or maybe I lost the ability to see it when it became too difficult to believe in. I know it's out there. He and I will find Montana someday.

MARCH 26, 1981

The President was shot four weeks ago tomorrow. Fortunately as history will tell he recovered but it really shook the nation. I was looking for a present for a baby shower when someone came out of the backroom and stated they had taken the President to the hospital. I asked for details and was so unsettled I went home and spent the rest of the day listening to news broadcasts.

America had its first flight of the space shuttle beginning two weeks ago today and landing the following Tuesday. It will be interesting to see what it brings to the future.

The first Sunday in March they realigned my stake and put my ex-husband and I in the same ward. It has promised to be an interesting arrangement.

My sister Jackie gave birth to her 3rd son on March 9. He was very healthy at 7 lbs 9 oz and is growing like a weed. He has lots of reddish blonde hair and looks like his daddy. They are going to name him Robert Nicholas Jenkins and call him Robbie.

On March 20 Ryan and I and Janet Kelly drove to California. On Sunday we went to the El Cajon 6th ward in El Cajon, just outside of San Diego. Monday we went to Sea World and the San Diego zoo. That night we went to the Mormon visitor center and saw Mr. Kruger's Christmas and a couple other Church films.

DISARRANGEMENT

The trip initially was to be Mom, Kathy, and me. With Kathy involved, the hotels that had been booked weren't your Motel 6 variety. When Kathy couldn't make the trip, things were downsized a bit. I was too distracted by my daydreams of Disneyland to notice. A room with a bed was just like any other room with a bed.

I had decided, being old enough to not believe in the costumed characters, that I'd prefer to cling to the riches of imagination. Looking past the seams and zippers, I mingled with fairytales. This allowed Disneyland to be a place where it was impossible to discern the difference between what was and what could be. That is the point of Disneyland—isn't it?

MARCH 26, 1981 CONTINUED

The next day we drove to Anaheim and went to Knott's Berry Farm and the Movieland Wax Museum. The next day we went to Disneyland. Thursday to Universal Studios and then planed to go to the Santa Monica Beach. It was so cold and windy I had to carry Ryan to the beach and made him stand in the ocean while I took our picture. Then we went to the Los Angeles Temple visitor center and took a tour and then watched movies.

INTO THE BREACH

There is a storm raging outside the car window and my Incredible Hulk plastic bucket and shovel are still tangled in the red, stretchy spider-webbing they were sold in. They will never be free to build sandcastles with moats meant to keep dragons at bay.

I'm not interested, but Mom is determined to run into the ocean. There might be rain but all I can feel is her hand around mine and the stinging sand as it slaps me from all directions. A photo, toes in the water, now quickly back to the shelter of the car.

Maybe she believes we'll never have a second chance. I'm hardly old enough to remember the experience and she's a year short of thirty. The significance of needing to touch the water to make the moment real is lost on me. I planned on returning to Disneyland the following week and every week after. The sea could wait until then.

MARCH 26, 1981 CONTINUED

The last day we went back to Disneyland and then drove to Las Vegas that night. It was a wonderful time. Ryan got to see Mickey Mouse, three times at Disneyland and along with the three little pigs, the big bad wolf, Winnie the Pooh, Chip (of Chip and Dale) and others. He was afraid of dark tunnels. We had to drag him on Peter Pan, Alice in Wonderland, Pirates of the Caribbean and others but he enjoyed them. He loves the "carnival rides" and had Janet and I sick at Knott's Berry Farm. He loved the corkscrew rollercoaster. The lights in Las Vegas really impressed him but the atmosphere was depressing.

PLAYING THE CROCODILE

Yes, there is a downside to believing everything at Disneyland is real. Not only is the happiest place on earth populated by princes and princesses, it also has an overwhelming number of villains lurking in the shadows. It would have been pointless to try and convince me that the Captain Hook, the Queen of Hearts, or any of the plundering pirates weren't real. I had already made up my mind. I do remember that getting me to enter Wonderland and the Caribbean wasn't nearly as difficult as risking a trip into Neverland. You could reason with me that the Queen of Hearts was only interested in blond-haired girls named Alice (my mother had brown hair and would not be mistaken for the troublesome young girl) and that the pirates were too busy looting to notice a small boy and his mother floating by in a boat. Captain Hook was an entirely different proposition. His life was dedicated to hunting down Peter Pan and the Lost Boys. As far as I was concerned, that was a group I had joined upon learning of its existence. If I wasn't the Peter Pan, I was most certainly a Peter Pan.

Mom, not knowing if or when we'd return, was determined to get me on the ride. How could her little Pan not see Neverland? So, being the intelligent and quick-witted woman that she is, she suggested that I pretended that I was the crocodile that swallowed Hook's hand. It was a stroke of devious brilliance. Tricking Hook into thinking I was a crocodile was a very Peter Pan thing to do. You see, not only had the crocodile taken Hook's hand—it had also swallowed a clock. If I simply said *tick tock* throughout the ride, Hook wouldn't dare come near me.

This story is told every time I return to Disneyland. I might even whisper a few *tick tocks* when Hook makes his appearances. I've still got plenty of Pan left in me and should there come a day when I've misplaced my mother, I will most certainly be lost.

SPACEBALL RICOCHET

Then there was Vegas, a convincing mirage of twitching lights promising a glance at something from a future world. It was magical, spectacular, and dazzling. Circus Circus, the name alone sent my heart and imagination racing. Clowns, elephants, ringleaders, lions, and tightrope walkers coming together for a three-ring spectacle.

I was disappointed to find that Circus Circus, despite its outward appearance, wasn't actually a massive tent. Still, I was blinded by the ringing bells, the crashing of coins as they fell from metal shoots into plastic buckets, women decked out in glimmering costume, circling the dimly lit rooms that seemed to ripple with life and mystery. Laughter, noise, laughter as the room spun. I stood small and at attention, staring up at the women on carousel horseback ascending into the hypnotic lights. It was decadence, had I known the word. The women in the sky were dropping balloons and suddenly I was not alone.

There was a scattering, shouts of glee as a stampede of adults converged. I was caught in a dust cloud of sharpened elbows and swinging hips—just like in the cartoons.

In their frantic over-play, the adults left me space. I watched as a shiny plastic bubble dropped from a rider's hand and floated down into mine. The thrill of the moment unsettled as the balloon was ripped away. A grown woman, short like my mother and nothing like my mother, looked through me with wide, hollow eyes. Vegas, the illusion and all its promises, broken.

JUNE 19, 1981

May and June are packed with birthdays and anniversaries and this year my sister Nanci graduated from high school (she will be at BYU in the fall). I had my 29th birthday, not the easiest, and Ryan had his 5th on June 9. My parents were down the first part of June and Ryan went camping with my father while they were here.

Today my sister Cristi had a baby boy. He was 4 weeks early and weighed only 5 pounds but they say he is doing very well. They are living in Seattle, Washington where her husband is doing graduate work in Pharmacology.

[We] had a birthday party for Jackie and David at Liberty Park. We walked through the aviary. The kids played on the swings etc. We ate watermelon and then we sent the children on a few rides. They decided they were too tame and wanted to go on the "tilt-a-whirl." I took Ryan and Scott; Jackie took Jeremy and Brandon. Everyone loved it but Scott. He clung to me after the first spin.

JULY 10, 1981

Terri had an 8 lbs 3 oz baby boy on June 21. They are naming him Dustin Matthew Carter. Terri, Scott and Dustin came and spent a week with us. Dustin is a real good baby and is growing up fast already. Scott and Ryan did more than their share of fighting yet when Ryan went to his dad's he had to call Scott and when Scott left on the airplane Ryan cried all the way home. Ryan had a brother for a few days.

Bruce and his fiancée Cheryl came down from Casper for the 4th of July. Cheryl is a real nice girl; she would make a good Mormon (she's Catholic). They are getting married October 10. While they were here they went to Temple Square and BYU. Hope to get to know her better.

Lately I've felt a little disenchanted with the institution of marriage. It seems there are so few good marriages and divorce is so rampant. The single life seems so much easier, but who knows.

THREE KIDS

I remember Kathy's house being something like The Ministry of Magic's Department of Mysteries, in that it seemed to be overflowing with strange, wonderful, and exotic items. It was easily as culturally diverse as the British Museum. The only real difference being that at Kathy's, there was a Planet of the Apes marathon on the television. If you could dream up a themed party, Kathy could reach into her cupboards of curiosities and make it come true.

My memories might be a little hyperbolic, but you could never convince me that Kathy's world wasn't the most interesting place in the galaxy. You could even find four-leaf clovers in her lawn. She made the impractical an essential part of our daily lives. If there was an adventure out there, Kathy would bring Mom and me to it.

In exchange, Mom would bring Kathy to church with us.

Church was a three-hour tour that felt infinitely longer. Kathy insists that she only came along because of the abundance of toys and treats my mother brought to keep me quiet. Kathy will downplay her sainthood, but if she came for playtime and snacks, she stayed because that was part of the balance that we all needed and shared.

In my mind, it was just like *Gilligan's Island* with less acrimony. Kathy was Ginger and my mother was Mary Ann. Kathy was more extravagant and elegant, Mom was more the girl-next-door type; they were both beautiful, passionate, determined, kind, and strong women.

I don't know exactly how I fit into the mix. I'd like to tell you that I played the same sort of role that Natalie Portman had in *Beautiful Girls* where she was the mature thirteen-year-old neighbor who sees herself as an "old soul." But I wasn't.

Kathy once told me, "You were smart, fairly well-behaved, and the most wonderful little boy in the world, but you were not mature."

What made Kathy and Mom so wonderful was that they still had a little bit of child left in them as well. Most importantly, they loved me and I never doubted that. Well, maybe just a little when they threw parties for their boyfriends that I wasn't invited to.

AUGUST 8, 1981

I saw John a few weeks ago. I invited him to dinner with me at Kathy's. Things went very well. I've talked to him twice since then. He was going to come to Salt Lake today and maybe stop and see me, but it must not have worked out. I'm seeing him next Saturday though. It seems so good to care about someone. It has been a long time.

My Relief Society job is really getting to me lately. We have little or no support for our activities. Our campout had to be cancelled this weekend, last week only one other person showed up, the same two weeks previously.

The activities give me a chance to contact the women and talk with them but the actual activities seem a waste of time, energy and expense. I'll see one of the Stake Presidency this week to renew my Temple Recommend and will talk with them; maybe they'll release me.

HOLLOW BONED

Returning home one Sunday afternoon from Church, my mother and I come across a wounded bird with a broken wing on the sidewalk. We rush home to get a box. I'm having visions of nursing the bird back to health with a little white sling and a twig for tiny crutch. When the wing healed, I imagine that the bird would come and visit from time to time. Maybe even build a nest on my windowsill. The was no trace of the bird when we returned. There was no need to punch three holes into the lid of the box anymore.

I've heard that bird migration patterns are instinctual and that new structures pose a threat to those who do not adapt. I don't know if there is any validity to that idea, but a few years ago, they replaced the parking lot next to where I live with an office building. A disturbing number of birds have died by colliding with 222 Main. I've never grown accustomed to seeing their ruffled-feather bodies waste away in the flowerbeds. The brown and black birds quickly blend in with the wood chips; the flamboyant-yellow strays take much longer. If I were smart, I'd stop looking for them, but to pass without acknowledging the loss of something beautiful feels disrespectful.

AUGUST 18, 1981

I saw John again on Friday night; it was a good evening. He took me to the Ho Ho Gourmet for dinner. The food was very good; the conversation was better. He has a way with questions, he asks a lot and they are seldom easy ones. He is such a caring and gentle person. During my marriage I buried my feelings so deep I worried that they would never surface again, but they are and it is great to be alive and feeling something.

Ryan goes in for Kindergarten testing this Friday and then starts school next Thursday. He is so excited and I'm proud, but it is hard to see him growing up so fast. I got his pants hemmed today; he's gotten taller this summer, but thinner.

I saw President Killpack this last week and talked to him about the Relief Society. He just smiled and told me he knew I would make the right decisions, but gave me no advice.

THE OUTSIDER

I thought that kindergarten would be a lot like daycare with personalized desks. It wasn't. There was something about the social structure that bewildered me. I wasn't really accustomed to making friends. I knew Jeff because my mother was assigned to look in on his mother. I don't remember having anything more than acquaintances at daycare. I don't think I spent my days off in an imaginary world, but it would make a lot of sense if I did. My aloof nature had to start somewhere, I just assumed that it was something I developed later in life.

There was a day early in the school year when a classmate brought some action figures from home to play with at recess. We were indoors that day, probably because of the weather. He had Dracula, Wolfman, and Gill-man (from *Creature from the Black Lagoon*) and I desperately wanted to play with them. He chose to share with another pair of boys. I couldn't understand why I hadn't been chosen. I don't know if the memory haunts me because of the action figures I didn't get to play with or because I suddenly realized I wasn't popular.

Mom and Kathy made me feel like I was the center of the universe. I didn't get everything I wanted, but I got my share. This wouldn't have been the first time that things didn't go my way; it was one of the first times that it mattered.

SEPTEMBER 13, 1981

Ryan has stared school. His teacher is Mrs. Prymeck. He has such enthusiasm for school. I hope it lasts. My sister Peggi had a baby girl on the 4th of September. She weighed 6 pounds 7 ounces and is really precious. They named her Nicole Marie. She is the first granddaughter on both sides of her family.

The last weekend of August Jackie and David, Kathy and I went down to Cedar City to see "Henry IV Part I" at the Shakespearean festival. It

was very good. I enjoyed the dancing and chamber music before the perfor-
mance and the apple tarts almost as much.

Terry, Mike, Scott, Dustin, Cheryl and Bruce were all down last weekend
and Mom and Dad were down this weekend. I've had a lot of company
this summer. We've all had good but hectic times.

I saw John again on Thursday. The more I know him the more I like him.
I worry that the relationship is going too fast. I guess I would like it to
last a long time and the way it is going we will be at the crossroads in no
time. I really enjoy the time we have together.

They still haven't released me from my calling. I talked to Brother
Harrison last night and he said they were looking, but not too hard.
Donita, who was supposed to take care of this Thursday, called, she can't
come. "Can she do it in 2 weeks?" Now what will we do this week? I'm
tired of worrying.

CARNIVAL SIDESHOW

I was born with two of my middle toes on my left foot webbed together up
to the first joint. I wasn't self-conscious about it. I never refused to go bare-
foot, fearing that someone might notice. It never occurred to me that being
different could be problematic.

On various occasions, I remember taking my sock off and proudly display-
ing my foot on the cold tile of the boy's restroom floor. For some reason, it
seemed inappropriate to do it elsewhere.

I don't know how it would come up in conversation. I imagine that I would
just blurt it out awkwardly whenever the time seemed right. It was something of a party trick, I suppose.

On at least one occasion, I took a Polaroid photo at home and brought it to school to show the girls in my class who expressed interest. Again, how my toes would come up in conversation is beyond me. This might be the strangest and most illogical thing I've ever done to try to impress someone. That's saying something. I suppose I thought that being unique would be of benefit.

Weirder still, I remember driving with my mother. It was grey and wet outside and I was worried about how she would identify my body if I were ever found dead somewhere.

"By your toes," she said.

That seemed perfectly reasonable.

Moments later, she'd ask if I wanted to have the toes separated. I took offense. No, I wasn't interested.

I am somewhat surprised that I never thought that my toes were evidence of some superpower, an alien origin, or both. I could have been an Olympic swimmer, if I had only seen myself differently.

Someone said, or I misconstrued, that Mormons on their missions weren't allowed to go swimming because the devil had dominion over the sea. It was my nature to be as fascinated as I was scared. So, while drawing a bath, I would stick my hand into the running water to test the theory.

NOVEMBER 13, 1981

Two months have passed since I last wrote. A lot has happened and yet a lot has not. I am still the chairwoman of the Relief Society. Our attendance has really dropped off and my heart isn't in it anymore. It seems I am trying to create a need that isn't there.

My grandfather Frank Earl Young age 82 died on October 25. He had been sick for so many years and it was a blessing for him to finally go. I flew back to Omaha for the funeral. He looked so good; it had been many years since I saw him without an expression of pain.

I have seen a lot more of John the last 2 months. I'm afraid I love him. He does not share my feelings. I love to talk to him; he makes me think and stretch myself a little. He asks questions no one else would dare ask and you feel you have no choice as to whether to answer honestly. I really enjoy his honesty although it may not always be as it is but as he sees it. He is strong and kind, but not perfect. I wish I could be more for him, but he needs to find his own way.

Bruce and Cheryl got married on October 12 in the Catholic Church in Casper. It was an experience for all of us. My youngest sister Nanci and I both came away convinced we would never marry outside the Church. It was very hard on my parents, especially my mother. Bruce and Cheryl are down in Corpus Christi, Texas for at least 3 months. I think it will do them good to be away from both families for a while.

Ryan is doing well in school. I went to his first parent teacher conference today. His teacher is pleased with his work, except his coloring. He is doing very well in mathematics. He really likes his teacher.

THE DRAW OF GUMBALLS

Every morning, a rather large group of us would set out from Murray Day School for McMillan Elementary, not allowed to cut across the neighbor's yard or stop anywhere along the way. The walk felt like a thousand miles, twisting through the neighborhood. You couldn't see the end from the beginning. There was a particular building that had been singled out as absolutely off-limits. It was nothing more than a small office building that stood direct-ly next to the school grounds, just beyond the chain-link fence. The building itself offered no temptation. The candy dispensers in the vestibule, however, they seemed to call out to the warm nickels in my pockets.

Some businessman who had forgotten what it is to be young must have complained about the noise of children clamoring around the gumball ma-chine. From the sidewalk, there didn't appear to be any discernable danger. Granted, candy had become an interesting topic. We had been taught that should anyone offer us candy, particularly if they were strangers, we were to refuse. Discerning which was more dangerous at the time, the people or their candy, I couldn't say. There seemed two options: kidnap or poison and neither were the least bit attractive to me. The last thing I wanted was my mother to have to identify my body because I had taken candy from a stranger.

One afternoon, I lingered behind. Without adult supervision, herding us back to daycare was never as efficient as it was organizing us in the morn-ing. Many classmates started back as soon as the bell rang. Others lagged behind. The gap between groups offered a window. If done quickly, I could infiltrate and escape the forbidden vestibule without being seen. I did not go alone—I was brave, but not nearly that bold. Maybe, I reasoned that should I be caught, it was safer to have someone who would take a percentage of the blame. Was I the instigator or the follower? I'm inclined to say the latter only because I was the more nervous. This was not my accomplice's first ven-ture into the vestibule.

I was disappointed to find that there were no spells or enchantments to keep us from simply swinging open the tinted glass door. It was just a brown and drab entryway. There was nothing but silence and an undeniable lack of ad-venture as I inserted my coins, turned the knob, took my candy, and ventured back out into the permissible world. Rule breaking wasn't nearly as much fun or rewarding as I had hoped it would be.

1982

JANUARY 10, 1982

A new year and a new resolve to do better, as usual, to keep a journal. The last few months have been difficult for me. The two years previous were good, no real ups or downs just life going along. Not a lot of turmoil in my own life. Last July I started dating John, someone I've cared for, rather admired from afar. I've wanted to know how I felt about him for a long time. I really expected that I had built him up in my mind and would be disappointed. But I wasn't disappointed. He is more than I expected. I have not seen a great deal of him, a lot less than I would like but my feelings for him have grown. For the past couple months I have felt a real love for him. His feelings do not seem nearly so deep. He says he cares and I think he does, although I think he wishes he didn't. He leads me to believe the reason he could never allow his feelings to grow is because he could never raise another man's son. I feel his reasons are probably different [and if they were] this would cause me less pain. I have seriously thought of ending the relationship but whenever I pray or attend the Temple I feel so good about the relationship. When we are together it is so good, but when we are apart is so hard for me. My bishop told me to be patient and I should be. I'm expecting miracles and even miracles sometimes take time. Sometimes in expecting or rather wanting so much I don't appreciate the things he does for me. For Christmas he brought me 2 books The Diary of Anne Frank and The Pleasures of Philosophy. He brought me another book last Friday to read. He says he cares and that I don't pester him too much. Although I often feel I do. I wish we could have an honest relationship but alas I think that is impossible. The rules seem to dictate that game playing is unavoidable. Today, if it isn't obvious, I am down. I love John but I am very unfulfilled by the relationship right now. I want to be loved. I realize John has to be careful and not to encourage me too much but I have no idea exactly where I stand with him.

Ryan and I had a very good Christmas. This is the first year I haven't had problems with the outlaws. This year they allowed Mike to take Ryan to their party and all went well.

I was privileged to attend the temple dedication of the Jordan River Temple in November. It was a spiritual experience and a blessing to be there. This was the second dedication I had been to. I attended the Provo dedication in 1972. When I got my recommend for the dedication my Bishop challenged me to ask John to pray with me. I really thought a suggestion of that kind would end the relationship but John agreed to pray and it was a good experience. Later that night we went to a wedding reception for a girl in my Relief Society. She had gotten married at the church [earlier in the day]. John commented on how temporary it all seemed. And it did. How I love him.

FEBRUARY 15, 1982

This last week I was involved with giving a baby shower for Patti Buck (who I work with). Ryan's class's Valentine Party (I'm a room mother) and the Stake Sweetheart Ball. Ryan and I also went to see Cottonwood High's production of Rumpelstiltskin and Macmillan Grade School had a patriotic program Ryan participated in. Everything went well. I asked John to go to the Sweethearts Ball with me and he did. I was really nervous how he would react. It never ceases to amaze me how adaptable and at ease he is in almost every situation. It was an "adult" dance and the average age attending had to be at least 50 and the music was 1940's but John is a good dancer, I'm poor but he didn't complain about his toes being smashed and we had a real good time. Later we seemed really close and before he left he asked if we could pray together. He asked for blessings on our relationship and help in the decisions we make and strength to respect each other. I felt very close to him. I care too much. He's the most caring and gentle person I have ever known and I've never been attracted to anyone as I am him.

APRIL 02, 1982

Last writing I was very encouraged about John and the relationship. February was wonderful. The week following (February 15) we had a Chinese New Year Party. Kathy, Gary (her boyfriend) John and I participated; we really had a lot of fun. Costumes, decorations, food, laughter. Everything went very well. Maybe too well. I don't know if John is just backing off a little or he is just very busy with other aspects of his life. He has been very tired and depressed and I haven't seen or talked much to him. His 35th birthday was yesterday, I sent him a bunch of balloons and a card. I care too much to let go.

Tomorrow opens General Conference. The news said they doubted President Kimball would attend. He has become very feeble. They stated he sometimes doesn't recognize his friends. The last time he was in the hospital I drew his blood; he looked very tired.

Last Saturday they had the women's session. The meeting was very good. A lot of emphasis on accepting yourself and your talents—not expecting to be perfect.

Ryan has his first loose tooth (bottom right front). He is so proud of it. I went to parent teacher conference last week. Mrs. Prymeck said he has really excelled the past 9 weeks. She said he had a real talent for math and getting along with others.

LOOSE ENDS

I remember standing outside my mother's bedroom with a string wrapped around my tooth and the other end tied to the door handle. The idea was that I could slam the door and it would pull out the tooth. Part of the memory is me telling myself that it was a bad idea and wasn't going to work. And it didn't work.

When I ask Mom about it, she laughs. She has vague memories of something like that happening, but suggests that it's something all kids do. She didn't, but all other kids do. Maybe I saw it on television or was convinced by my cousin Jeremy that this was the most efficient way to get the tooth fairy to leave a dollar under my pillow. He was a year older than me. That's like a decade in kid years. If that's the case, my tooth might not have actually been loose in the first place.

MAY 5, 1982

My parents were [here] for Easter. Ryan had a good time making Easter baskets for his grandparents. Easter morning I went down to Pleasant Grove to deliver an Easter basket to John. I went at 5:00 so I could be back by 6:30. I thought I had been by his house before but when I got there I realized I had been to a relative's. All of the maps of the town had been torn out of the phonebooks and I spent about 45 minutes looking over the town. I finally went down to State Street and found a phonebook with a map. I drove back to town and to his house. It was light by then and I was afraid of being caught, but I wasn't. By the time I got home it was about 7:15 and Ryan was up and had his Easter basket. He made his grandparents go to their room while he got their baskets. He was more excited about their basket than his.

The next Sunday Terri and family arrived and stayed a week. Monday we went to Chuck E Cheese Pizza Time Theater for family home night. During the week we all went roller skating and rented a video machine and watched movies another night.

Between visits from my family Kath and I had a M*A*S*H party. We dressed in army clothes and had dinner in a tent pitched over at the church and then watched the movie M*A*S*H over at Kathy's. Gary and John came and we had a good time. After the movie John came over to my house and slept while I watched a movie and then he went home.

DRESSING UP'S WASTED ON PRINCES

Reading Mom's journal entries, particularly those featuring Charming, is akin to watching a horror film where the audience sees the impending consequences of the choice the character is about to make. You can shout and scream all you want; it won't change anything. I know because I did shout and scream as it unfolded before five-year-old me.

Every act of kindness from Charming came laced in venom. It was abundantly clear to Kathy that in his mind, there wasn't enough room in the world for both him and me. Mom focused on the positives and made sure I was at my father's whenever she expected to see him.

To keep me from feeling entirely left out, Mom and Kathy would often throw a pre-party for me. I still felt unjustifiably exiled. Charming had no appreciation for dressing up. He acted like his kimono or medical scrubs were straightjackets. He had to be talked into doing everything.

MAY 5, 1982 CONTINUED

Last Saturday night John came up to attend a wedding reception with me. Mike was busy and couldn't take Ryan so I got a babysitter. John came to dinner and Ryan ate with us. I fixed spaghetti because I thought Ryan would eat it, he wouldn't and John doesn't like spaghetti—great start. Ryan was a bit sassy at dinner. I chose to ignore it wishing to keep the meal enjoyable but I should have disciplined him more as he got worse and I was glad when dinner was over. Ryan went in to watch an animated special on TV and I went to get Mitch Ricks (my cousin) to babysit. John stayed with Ryan. When I got back Ryan and John had been fighting and it set a bad tone for the rest of the night. Later I tried to talk about my feelings and things ended rather sad. It is really a turning point in our relationship, if we make it through this… I do love him and I hurt at the thought of never seeing him again.

A POUND OF FLESH

I didn't know that I had been weaponized, that I was Charming's go-to excuse. It incenses me now—would have destroyed me then. I knew that the relationship hadn't progressed as Mom had hoped. I didn't want to the reason that she didn't get what she wanted.

I had never been a bad child, just a little mouthy, unable to always bite my tongue. Rarely would I willfully go against Mom's wishes. When I did, she didn't like grounding me because she felt I already spent too much time on my own. Instead, she started to take away my weekly allowance.

Charming was bad for the economy; he brought out the worst out in me.

Mom didn't confide in me how much she wanted him to love her, but I knew. Disappointment was something I recognized. I had been there as she planned the parties, made endless phone calls to various stores looking for a particular item, and drove across town to pick up the gifts. I was there when she put her heart into the baskets.

I also knew that her efforts meant very little to Charming because Mom was never as happy after the dates as she was while preparing them. I was envious, like any child would be, but most of all, I was just angry.

I knew that on this particular occasion, Mom's trust in me was betrayed. Sometimes, saying exactly what I felt was a mistake. Sometimes, it was well worth the fine.

Charming and I had a fistfight. I'm sure I threw the punches but I promise you it wasn't unprovoked. He liked to push my buttons because he believed he was untouchable. I had to show him my arms weren't nearly as short or as weak as he thought they were.

If he was going to throw down his gauntlet, he had to know I would take it up.

The problem was that Mom loved him. Or at least, she thought she did. Someone had to apologize and it wasn't ever going to be him. I was as selfish and self-centered as the next kid, but when it came to Mom, I'd say whatever would make her happy and try my best to mean it. Maybe it was something I learned from my father.

MAY 10, 1982

The last week has been hard for Ryan and I. Ryan decided to write and tell John he was sorry. Kathy said she would help him write it so I couldn't edit it. She kept putting it off so Saturday afternoon I sat down with Ryan and let him write what he wanted:

Dear John, I am sorry that I said I hate you. Come back when you can. Love, Ryan.

I only did a little bit of editing; he wanted to ask him to come back tomorrow. I talked him into "when you can."

I talked to my mother last night for Mother's Day. She sounded lonely and worried about me, as usual.

Yesterday my Bishop called me in. The stake president has asked him to find out about Mike. After 4 years they are going to do something. I don't know what will happen but...

All in all it was a bittersweet Mother's Day. Ryan made me a card and a poster and an emergency kit (needle, thread, pins, band aids) and he looked so cute singing in the Mother's Day program.

MY FATHER'S ARCHIVES

There is a box in Mom's basement, medium in size, torn by love on one side and barely able to keep its contents, with "Ryan's special box" scribbled across the top. Inside are three yearbooks, Halloween decorations, papier-mâché art, children's books, a few photographs of me, hundreds of scribble and scratch drawings, and a vinyl pouch that contains multiple copies of my father's obituary and the register from his funeral. In the physical, sense this is what remains of my father's life and most of it is about or by me. Herein are snippets of peace, the slightest of comforts, and a rush of the quiet warmth that dominated the few hours a week we spent together. No traces of pain, just misspelled words that combine to say: Daddy, I love you.

JUNE 5, 1982

Celebrated my 30th birthday on May 29th. It was a little hard. The day before I was feeling very blue. I decided to go buy me a new outfit to make me feel better. At the store everything looked ugly so I decided I must be middle aged which made me feel worse. While wandering around the mall I ran into Kathy and Dan. They took me to Ferrell's for ice cream and I felt better.

The next day I worked in the yard in the morning. That afternoon my parents came from Wyoming on their way to Seattle to visit Cristi and Wayne. My parents got to meet John when he came to pick me up for a picnic with Kathy, Sue and Dan. We went to Murray Park and had a good time. John and Dan talked us out of going roller-skating so we went back to Kathy's and talked for a while. It was a good birthday.

Ryan made me a birthday cake and decorated it (with Kathy's help) so we took that to my sister Jackie's on Sunday and had a party there.

John and I had a good time and did no serious talking. But I feel he still cares and I know I still do.

Ryan will be 6 in 3 days! He has lost one tooth (April 11) and has another real loose one. His father bought him a bike. He looks so grown up riding it.

WATER LUNG

I remember being five or so, I'm bobbing up and down in the swimming pool that sit lazily in the middle of father's condominium complex. The pool is full of enough people that a boy could get lost in the commotion. The sun is blinding bright, bleaching away the color of the hot summer day. My father is watching from the side, taking in the sun. He always liked to have a tan; in the winter months, you'd find him under a hot lamp in the bathroom. There is no warning as I slip from the inflatable doughnut and watch the water close above me. The sun shimmers like confetti on the surface as the water slips through my lips. Someone pulls me up from the water.

There's something strangely cinematic about this memory. Not only in its beauty, but also in the sense of calm detachment I feel in retelling it. I know the moment is real and that for a time, it haunted me. I'd watched enough news to know that sometimes children went into the water and never came out.

JUNE 27, 1982

Ryan had a great birthday. He chose to have his party at McDonald's and I was really surprised at the quality of party they put on. Ryan had a good time and was delighted with his party. Two days later he lost his second tooth. His teacher at nursery school pulled it out for him.

MCBIRTHDAY

It really was a brilliant birthday, the sort you'd see in a movie. There was a separate building behind the McDonald's near Cottonwood Mall that housed parties. Even the main restaurant had a giant talking tree in the middle and was designed in a shiny-plastic-playground style. It wasn't terribly far from where we lived and was one of my favorite places to go eat. The birthday building was even more elaborate, an amusement-park wonderland full of McDonald's characters with that perfect anime-in-real-life candy coloring. The Hamburglar, Birdie, Grimace, and Ronald McDonald himself were all represented. Ronald, some poor young adult in a clown suit with painted red smile and matching wig, even came by in the flesh. I remember a train ride, a small theater, and a roomful of Happy Meal toys for me to choose from.

JUNE 27, 1982 CONTINUED

Ryan and his father have had their picture in Utah Holiday magazine advertising Fashion Place Mall this month. It was a nice picture. They also did a TV commercial for Father's Day. Ryan saw it while he was at nursery school. I never got to see it.

A THOUSAND WORDS

The forecast is rain. A man is debating if it is appropriate for my father and me to wear hats indoors. "It's not historically accurate," he says. "It looks better if they wear hats," someone else says.

There's an antique tube radio, which the entire scene seems to be built around, and fancy a chair, softer and a little more worn than those my father owned. I don't remember anyone ever actually sitting in the chairs that my father owned.

They're checking the lighting; to me it just feels like they're dragging their feet.

Most of the day, we sat in the less ornate kitchen with its contemporary appliances shoehorned into the turn-of-the-century floorplan. The door leading to the backyard is open. Outside it's grey, there are garden plots and rain-ruined plans. We're dressed up like Sunday morning 1931 in an attempt to stir a whiff of a yesteryear we'd never know.

My father and I are cast in the familiar roles of father and son for a Father's Day print ad and television spot for Fashion Place Mall. We're somewhere in the eastern bench of Salt Lake City where all the streets are named after prestigious universities.

We wear hats in the living room. I sit on my father's lap as the flashbulbs pop. The lighting is bright and hot, but in print it will appear warm and inviting.

Later, I would sneak around a reclining chair in a more spacious room dressed in a contemporary style and surprise my father with a small box that contained the mundane gift of socks.

I'm puzzled by how the photographs and the video aspects fit together thematically.

I saw the television ad once. I was at daycare, which would seem like the ideal place to garner the proper amount of awe from my peers. They were anything but starstruck. There had been a bit stapled on the end of the advertisement that featured a man dressed in a jester suit. Everyone wanted to know if I had met the man in the costume. I had to confess I hadn't, which disappointed them and that disappointed me.

Mom would never see the commercial and years later, when she tried to get a copy from Fashion Place Mall, they told her that they had just recently thrown their archives away.

I wonder what it would be like to watch my father move. There are no home movies to flicker against a wall to show me his gait. Just still life.

FEAR AND LOATHING IN RAPID CITY

Later in June, Mom and I set out on a road trip with her sister Terri's family, their brother Bruce and his wife, Cheryl. The voyage took us to Rapid City, South Dakota to see Mount Rushmore. I was not impressed. It looked the same, if not better, on TV. Mom remembers feeding the chipmunks. Mom always feeds the chipmunks.

I don't know if I realized how close we were to Montana. Not that I would have wanted to go there without Dad. I had a feeling that Montana couldn't exist without my father. It was a place behind a magic door that only opened for the two of us.

Had I known the truth, that the land he owned was actually part of the polygamist compound that his old roommate Jon had run off to, I might not have seen it as paradise.

I wonder if my father ever went to visit the land he helped purchase or if he believed polygamy could change a man? Did he think of Montana as a magical neverland, like I did?

If he did go, he wouldn't have found the place he was searching for.

Jon claimed that by joining the polygamist sect and withdrawing from the mainstream world he had been "cured" of his same-sex attraction. Did my father look at Jon with a sense of envy or pity? Having multiple wives wouldn't have changed him. So many honeymoons and never enough closet space.

Our Montana wasn't a place where Dad would go and play straight. It was a world where he didn't have to pretend to be anything.

On that vacation, our merry band of fools would visit Flintstones Bedrock City, which I remember being a lot of concrete and not remotely as impressive as Disneyland, and Reptile Gardens, where it was rumored that they would put a bumper sticker on your car unless you specifically asked them not to.

Inside Reptile Gardens was a vast collection of reptiles and exotic plants. There was a show that featured chickens on roller skates, a farmyard with miniature ponies, and an area with giant tortoises and snakes. Mom held a snake so I figured it couldn't be too dangerous and agreed to do the same. This is the same woman that taught me to pet the giant fuzzy bumblebees as if they were tiny cats. I survived as the snake started out around my shoulders, slid its way down to my waist, wrapped around my leg, and slithered away.

The highlight of our visit was the funhouse mirrors. I'm not sure what they had to do with reptiles but Mom and I could have spent hours just laughing at each other's distorted reflections. We left knowing the size we came in was preferable to taller, wider, shorter, or thinner version of ourselves.

When we returned to the car, I was disappointed to see that we had escaped without a bumper sticker. From there, we visited Dinosaur Park before heading back towards Wyoming where Mom and I separated from the rest of the pack to visit Yellowstone Park. I was fascinated that the geysers functioned on a regular schedule. Mom found chipmunks and squirrels to feed.

We spent the night in Jackson Hole before driving through Star Valley. This proved to be the biggest letdown of the entire trip. I had envisioned a valley filled with a sea of diamonds glittering light. Little by little, I was learning to expect less from life.

When we returned home, Mom was supposed to see Charming. He claimed he was sick.

JUNE 30, 1982

I went down to see John today. I had checked out a book on plastic surgery for him. I had made cookies to send to the missionaries and I took some to him also. When I got there he was busy with an emergency surgery so didn't see much of him; but it was worth the wait.

Ryan and I went to see Annie yesterday. We enjoyed it. As we left I threw my keys into the garbage and ended up going through the basket; yucky.

FLOWERS FROM MARS

My mother had a small garden boxed into the back corner of our yard in Murray. It wasn't particularly typical of suburbia, nor was it designed to provide sustenance. It was, however, essential in my mother's idea of what a home was. We'd always have a small garden for tomatoes, cucumbers, carrots, and the occasional experimental pumpkin patch. Once upon a time, there were sunflowers that were twice my height with long slender stems bending at the neck, barely able to lift their fire-framed heads. They fascinate me more in the memory than they did when I stood before them, armed with an armada of rebel scum and the Galactic Empire. They were beautiful and unlike anything else in the neighborhood—just like my mother and me. We were not on the verge of extinction; we were a rarity about to become a common occurrence.

JULY 11, 1982

Already July! Ryan and I had a good 4ᵗʰ of July weekend. Saturday the 3rd Ryan went swimming at his dad's and I stayed home and grimaced as they brought our piano up two flights of stairs. Ryan came home around 12 and we had lunch and then went to see E.T. with Jackie, David, Jeremy and Brandon; Robbie stayed with a babysitter. The show was good; I cried so hard I left with a terrible headache and puffy eyes. Ryan enjoyed it too. Then we went to the Jenkins for Kentucky Fried Chicken and watermelon. After it got dark we set off fireworks, ground sparklers and roman candles and the kids did some sparklers. We got home about 11p.m.

LOVING THE ALIEN

I remember seeing *Close Encounters of the Third Kind* sometime in my youth and not being able to connect with it. It was too cerebral and didn't make any sense to me. Fortunately *E.T. the Extra-Terrestrial* wasn't about brains; it was about heart. I connected with Elliott's loneliness and his desperate need to be special. I didn't realize that this was a universal need that all children feel. I doubt I even understood what exactly it was that I loved about the film. I do know that my favorite scene has always been the unleashing of the frogs. Specifically, Elliott's skillful use of a chair to steal a kiss amidst the chaos.

JULY 11, 1982 CONTINUED

They had called me earlier in the day to tell me that Ryan had a talk to give [at church the next morning]. There hadn't been much time on Saturday to prepare. I had made a trip to the library and looked through [copies of the LDS published magazine] Children's Friend. I picked out a poem but there really hadn't been time to practice so after I found some pictures and composed a simple sentence about each picture with a patriotic theme. Ryan got up the next morning determined to stay home from Primary. He would not give a talk. With a 9 a.m. Primary I didn't have too much time to convince him and get some practice in but we did get through it several times. As we entered Primary the president approached us and exclaimed how good it was to have Ryan there and ready for his talk. He immediately hid behind me and she commented that she knew he was shy and he presently turned at least three times shyer. He consented to sit on the stage but when it was time for his talk he refused to get up. I came up and he came to stand next to me, but behind the pulpit. I handed him the first picture but he wouldn't say a word. As an in-front-of-audience compromise I gave the talk and he held out the pictures (still hiding behind the pulpit). Ryan's first talk.

A CHILD IN THE HOUSE OF GOD

Going to church was a strange, often boring experience. It didn't feel necessary like daycare. We didn't have to be there in our tight shoes and button-up shirts that grabbed at our necks. We could have been outside at a park, in the backyard saving a princess, or watching TV. It was impossible to sit still on the hardwood pews. They certainly weren't designed for comfort.

After the hour-long sacrament meeting, the children would be separated from their parents like the wheat from the weeds. We would then be filtered into various classrooms based on our age for another hour and then finish with all the children together to sing songs and listen to other children stumble through talks that had been written by their parents.

My imagination led me to believe that the adults were separated from the children so that they could have a more enjoyable experience that included very little lecture, reverence, or any of the quiet behavior that they continually stressed in our classes.

There was a large, rectangle-shaped part of the chapel's ceiling that I thought would swing open when no children were present and open a gate to hell. My version of hell was like a scene from *Haxan: Witchcraft through the Ages,* a surreal European film from 1922, or an Oingo Boingo music video: campy, melodramatic, and filled with people dressed in cheap monster costumes dancing around a fire.

For a while, my mom taught a class. It was for kids who were a year or two older than I was. Rather than fighting with me every week, she let me tag along. Once she was released and someone else took over the class, I was forced to play by the rules. Primary became a difficult place for me to go without my mother.

The struggle of getting me to go to class lasted until one of the young women in the Primary Presidency told me she loved me. Her love was enough to make me want to go each week to see her. To be loved is a glorious thing.

Love, however, was not enough motivation to convince me speaking in front of my peers was a good idea. It promised catastrophic collapse and embarrassment. Some found my shyness to be cute; I played to that.

Fortunately, none of the other kids were about to say anything. They could be asked to speak the following week.

JULY 11, 1982 CONTINUED

In Sacrament Meeting for the closing song we sang "The Star Spangled Banner." As they played an introduction Ryan grabbed his flag (part of his talk) and stood up with his hand on heart. It brought me to tears.

I had to work on the 5th of July, the official holiday and Mike couldn't take Ryan so Sunday night I took him out to my sister Jackie's. It rained most of the day so they stayed home and I picked Ryan up after work and came home planning on lots of sleep. Ryan really wanted to see the fireworks and Kathy helped convince me I needed to go. So we walked over to Murray Park and watched a program and then a very nice fireworks display and got home about 11 p.m.

The morning of the 6th I got up at 2 a.m. to see the eclipse of the moon. I'm afraid I didn't enjoy it as much as those who stayed up the whole night to see it start to finish but I did get a glance. What impressed me was how dark it was outside, but the stars were out.

The rest of the week was routine. I talked to John on Wednesday and he is planning on coming up Saturday for our lab picnic.

THE POWER OF TWO

When Mom worked and my father couldn't take me, I spent my weekend nights sleeping next to my cousin Jeremy, Jackie's son. He was a year older than me—the top of the food chain as far as grandchildren and cousins went. I was his second, a sidekick filled with naïveté, which made me the perfect accomplice.

Jeremy was better at being mischievous; he had younger brothers to practice his trade upon. This isn't to suggest that I didn't contribute to our adventures or that I wasn't a willing participant. I just wasn't the one in charge.

In one of his more baffling feats, Jeremy burned down the kitchen while trying to determine what would happen if he tried to cook a puzzle piece in the oven. My opinion wasn't asked for; I wasn't there.

Our imaginations were matched only by our ambitions. How many dreams did we scheme in the darkness between bedtime and sleep? A thousand? Yes, and a million more. The lights of passing cars stretched across the walls and slid away into the darkness as we hoped for alien abduction. We were little boys destined to be ghostbusters, Jedi, superheroes and kings. We feared only the inevitable normality of our lives.

We fought our share, but even a good day could bring bloody noses and scraped knees; neither the disagreements nor the bruises remain.

We built a snack shop—a glorified lemonade stand. It was going to make us millions. We didn't realize that would require us to sell billions of already overpriced drinks and candy. We should have also offered a movie.

Summer nights were often spent sleeping in the backyard on the trampoline even though I knew my allergies would cause a bloody nose by morning. We made elaborate plans for snow forts inspired by Disney cartoons that we were never able to build to spec, but we did try.

Some nights, we'd travel to places far away. I was the power from which a signal was created and Jeremy was the eyes to translate our travels. Without the other, our powers were useless. Together, we walked through mansions, exotic playgrounds, and tiptoed through the bedrooms of our secret crushes in search of evidence that might suggest a happily ever after.

Jeremy, you needn't say anything; I know it was real.

After my father's death, Jeremy was often there, still and quiet in the dark next to me as I cried myself to sleep. Sometimes he knew, often he didn't. Eventually, I learned to cry in silence.

Jeremy had a younger brother, Brandon, but he was paired up with my other cousin Scott, Terri's son, who was born around the same time. Then Robbie (not just a childhood twist on Robert, to this day we refer to him as Robbie) came along, he was the third son in Jeremy's family and teamed up with Dustin, Scott's younger brother. Three pairs, six misfits, until Jackie had to go and have another son, Cameron. Cameron was on his own. I'm always somewhat surprised to see him these days, not just because he survived but because he isn't the four-year-old anymore. How could he grow up when his role seemed so permanent? I suppose it is his right, his parole.

For all the trouble we caused, come Christmas, the parents would exact their revenge by dressing us up as various characters from the nativity and videotaping us as we stumbled about in oversized turbans, potato bags turned into shepherd robes, and tinsel haloes. We'd gather around an old plastic doll meant to be Jesus while someone read from the Bible. It was as dysfunctional as anything you're likely to see dramatized on television and we loved it. Particularly when we added a wooly sheep with wooden legs and a voice box that baa'd when you tipped it upside down.

One year, our program took on a more secular theme and saw us dressing up as elves with green tights, red felt tunics, and pointy hats. Dustin was dressed as a pre-adolescent Santa Claus who burst through the workshop doors to wish everyone a merry Christmas. We took to our roles with such gusto you'd think we didn't realize that in ten years this was going to be blackmail.

Following the performance was the white elephant gift extravaganza where the standard of the perfect gift was set by my mother's contribution of "potty pot shots" (toilet target practice). The night would end with cupcakes with little plastic nativity scenes on them to be eaten once we finished a rousing chorus of "Happy Birthday" for Baby Jesus.

AUGUST 10, 1982

The last month has been another busy one. John did not make it up for the lab's party. I was disappointed, but I really can't compete with his practice. The week before my Grandmother Young came from Omaha by way of Casper for a short visit. Thursday night we went down to Steve and Peggi's and John came too. We had supper and then walked down to the park for a few minutes. Ryan, Grandma and I went on a quick tour of BYU before we went back to Salt Lake City. Grandma and I went shopping on Thursday and again on Friday. Then we took her to the airport on Friday afternoon. It was a good visit for all of us. She got a picture of John and I that she is very proud of.

The next weekend (July 22-25) I went to Cedar City with my neighbors Kathy and Sue and Kathy's mother to attend the Shakespearean Festival. We saw "As You like It," "Romeo and Juliet" and "Henry IV Part II." They were all very good and we had a good time. Ryan stayed at home with his dad. They went to the 24th of July parade and a couple shows (Star Trek and E.T.). He stayed part of the time at Lynne and Tim's.

DATING WITH DAD

On one occasion, I remember tagging along with my father on a date. It was a seemingly nondescript evening that took place in a gentleman's condo. There was a dim and warm glow that reflected off the long mirrors of the dining area and stretched to reach into a living room as the sun set. I don't remember eating; I assume we did. I also don't remember our host's face. It is almost as if he wasn't a person as much as he was a form, another uncredited extra without distinction. The most memorable aspect of the evening found my father and this date on the couch and me at their feet watching *Star Trek: The Motion Picture* (on the nearly forgotten RCA CED format that Grandma Gloria also had). I had selected the film from a stack of long forgotten titles and while I'm not sure what my other choices were, I assume that my love for *Star Wars* influenced my selection. This would be my introduction to Captain Kirk, et al. I don't know if I liked the film; I don't really remember much beyond the blurring lights of opening credits. Maybe I, like many others, fell asleep at that point. I also don't remember ever seeing my father's date again.

The only other film I know that I saw with my father was Sylvester Stallone in *First Blood*. I don't actually recall seeing the film with my father. I assume that this was also a date because taking his six-year-old to an R-rated movie wasn't exactly in my father's character.

What I remember is sitting on my mother's bed while she read the newspaper on the floor below me. Looking over her shoulder, I saw an ad for *First Blood* and commented that my father had taken me to see it. I kept nothing from her and my father never asked me to. If I happened to drop the occasional bombshell, it was purely accidental.

AUGUST 10, 1982 CONTINUED

The next weekend Ryan and I went to the Fisher Family reunion (my mother's family) at Island Park in Idaho. It is my grandmother's 85th birthday and she promised that she wouldn't have another if I didn't attend. Mom, Dad, Jackie, David and boys, Terri, Mike and boys and Ryan and I shared a "cabin." We did a little exploring, floating on the river in a rubber raft and the men folk fished a little. Saturday night we met with everyone and had the party for grandma with singing around the campfire. We traveled back Sunday morning.

Sunday night John came up and we had dinner at Kathy's with Dan. Then we went for a walk and talked. John also played the piano and sang for me. He's quite impressive but I'm very partial.

Last night Ryan and I went down to Provo to celebrate Peggi's birthday. After her party I stopped by John's office to pick up a plate and leave him some old magazines. There was a note that said to call him. I first called his home and his father told me he was at his sister Nancy's. I called him there and he said his mother wanted to meet me. So I agreed to meet him at his home. After I got off the phone I told Ryan if he had ever been good *that he had better be good or else. As we drove he asked me to be quiet and he prayed that he would be able to be good. We arrived at John's when he did. We met his father in the yard and then his mother in the house. We had a real nice conversation and Ryan behaved himself fairly well. John's brother Mark stopped by and teased and entertained Ryan. I couldn't believe how tall he was! John's parents were very nice—really. His father has beautiful silver hair and was very friendly. His mother wasn't feeling well but she seemed a very genuine person and a very loving one. I was excited to meet them and they didn't disappoint me. They were very comfortable to be around.*

PARKSIDE

I switched schools following kindergarten. I had stopped attending Murray Day Care and Mom wanted me to forge friendships with people who lived closer to us. My new school, Parkside Elementary, is still located on the edge of Murray Park. The park was full of large, grassy hills where families gathered to strap themselves to large blocks of ice and race their way to the bottom. There were rivers for skipping rocks, a canopy of trees at the one end and thinning out the closer you came to the school, soccer fields, concrete igloos, wooden fortresses, a large baseball diamond with a sizeable grandstand, an old military airplane, and a thousand places for a child to hide—ninety percent of which were completely and absolutely off-limits during recess. We were forbidden to extend beyond the soccer field and a tree that seemed arbitrarily picked as the end of the world. There was a playground of wooden pedestals a hundred yards or so beyond our allowed borders. To reach this playground was the great new temptation and the way to prove oneself to be foolishly brave. Being terribly adventurous and regretfully brave, I know I ran past the tree, sometimes stretching out to the playground on various occasions. The first time being the most difficult, watching for whatever danger might be lurking, breathing in deep, and launching out in a run. The task became easier with each attempt until I either became bored with the trek or wised up to the protective reasons to stay closer to the school.

The giant steel airplane was always my favorite, but far from the school. From time to time, our teachers would take us there. More often, I visited this area of the park with my mother. The extended family would sometimes picnic there and I would have to fight my determined cousins to climb the wings. Looking back, it was terribly dangerous with a thousand ways to fall from the smooth metal wings. There was loose wiring protruding from the torn-up panels in the cockpit and sharp corners where wear and exuberant children had ripped the metal. It was almost as if it had fallen from the sky, lost and left to decay. But it had flown—this wasn't a cardboard playset or a child's stripped-bare version—this was the real thing. The cockpit was the place to be and, as a consequence, always the hardest place to get to. From there, the world would fade away as the skies became the ground I walked on. It wasn't an X-Wing fighter but it was close enough.

AUGUST 26, 1982

Today was Ryan's first day of first grade. Ryan was sad to leave nursery school; he took cookies for everyone yesterday. Last night he shivered and shook over going to a new school. When we got to Parkside School he clung to me like glue. We found his name on Mrs. Powers' class roster. After the bell we gathered around her as she read off the names. She read off Ryan's name and he slipped right into the room and into his desk and never looked back. I was the one left lost. I stood in the hall waiting for who knows what, wandered around a little and finally went home still feeling purposeless. I puttered the morning away, went to the grocery store and to a fabric store to start my Christmas shopping. At about 3:25 I arrived to pick Ryan up—no students. From the principal I learned that they had been let out an hour early. I panicked. I talked to the janitor—he told me he had seen someone out front—not Ryan. I talked to his teacher, she looked through the files to see if anyone lived near us—none. I went back to the car to look for him. We had walked to Murray Park a couple of times but I didn't think he knew his way home. As I drove back I was nearly home when I saw him walking through the cemetery. He wasn't nearly as concerned as I was. I called his school and let them know he was okay. About a half hour later his teacher called to find out if he was found. He had had a good day at school and is looking forward to returning tomorrow.

CHILD CROSSING

I didn't like changes to my daily routine, but I had learned that life often required you to adapt. I'd fret and worry, but when it came time to be brave and jump into the situation, I pulled myself together and put on the most stoic face I could muster.

On the first day of first grade, my mom dropped me off at my new school, promising to pick me up at the conclusion of classes. When we were sent home for the day and Mom wasn't there, I didn't panic. Simply assuming the adult world had taken her attention, I set out to walk home. It wasn't a difficult path to take—Mom and I had walked home from the park before and I knew the way.

Through to the edge of the park, cross the street, head up the hill, push on to the cemetery across from the abandoned movie drive-in, to the church, and then two blocks to home. I was somewhere between the top of the hill and the cemetery, probably by the old milk factory, when a car pulled over.

"Hey kid, you need a ride?"

Open daylight, cars racing past. I had made it this far; I was disinterested in a ride. I didn't want anyone's help. I could do this on my own. Besides, who were these people, why were they offering to give me a ride? Couldn't they be bothered to lure me in with candy? I was six years old, not stupid, and certainly not about to just get into someone's car. I didn't even look at them, simply said *no* and kept on walking.

Five minutes later, I was at the south edge of the cemetery. My pace had slowed; I liked to look at the headstones that had pictures. It seemed disrespectful to not stop and acknowledge them. Why else were they there? Most were of older adults, grandmas and grandpas, but I was more fascinated with the children. That's when Mom pulled up. She seemed panicked, but clearly happy to see me. I got into the car and we drove the last two blocks home.

SEPTEMBER 19, 1982

Almost another month gone by. Ryan is doing well in school. They had an abundance of second graders so they formed a combination first and second class. Ryan's teacher is taking that class so Ryan was moved into Mrs. Brennan's class. He didn't seem bothered by the move. Robbie Marshall (live around the block) is also in the class.

Two weeks ago I was called into the Stake President's office to talk over Mike and the divorce. It was harder than I thought it would be. I talked to Mike about making an appointment and going in to clear things up—but of course he won't. He claims he has nothing to hide and his only desire is to remarry—but I'm not convinced. He is still very adamant about his rights with Ryan.

MATHEMATICAL EXILE

In first or second grade (my mother insists it was in third, but that doesn't make any sense to me), the powers that be at Parkside Elementary decided to form an experimental math class. We were told that the participants would be selected randomly and that our aptitude for math would not be a factor. You can say that all you want but when a child sees all his friends selected and finds himself on the outside staring in, words like "random" translate into "you're simply not good enough."

I haven't a clue to exactly what the class consisted of. There were wooden blocks: red, yellow, blue, and green, and regardless of the difficulty level, playing with blocks was clearly better than scribbling in pencil. I never asked any of my friends about the course; I didn't want to know about all the fun I was missing.

In my mind, I never enjoyed math except for the two or three times we were given fake money (you had to punch out the bills and coins from a thin cardboard page at the back of your math book) in an effort to teach us how math translated into the world outside—the adult world. However, I've been told, and I struggle to believe, that I was actually rather good at math. It was my handwriting, spelling, and generally English that I found more difficult.

OCTOBER 16, 1982

I have seen more of John this month than usual. I picked apples and pears with him and went on house calls and to a nursing home with him one Saturday. He came to my sister Jackie's for dinner on Conference Sunday. He and Ryan got along very well. I was very nervous but they did splendid.

We had a lot of rain last month and there was quite a bit of flooding in Murray. I had water in my basement and if they hadn't used swamp pumps in my backyard I would have had a lot more.

John is in New York City now. He is cheering up his sister and attending a melanoma conference. He will come back a week from tomorrow.

Ryan is really enjoying school. He is beginning to read and just loves it. He is such a good boy, only rarely gives me any concern.

I have been busy making Halloween costumes. Ryan will be a pirate, I'm a witch and I borrowed David's clown suit for John.

OCTOBER 28, 1982

Ryan and I went to the Halloween party and had a really good time. Ryan was a good kid and I really appreciated it.

Things have gone well for John and me this last month. I have seen a lot of him and although we have our problems I feel very confident.

Ryan has been learning a lot at school. He is really progressing in reading and math. At parent-teacher conference Ryan's teacher said he was doing really well and was an ideal pupil in class. He has lots of friends and enjoys school. We have been through a bit of sex education this past month; it is just amazing what a 6-year-old can bring home from school.

My parents came down for Thanksgiving. It was good to see them and talk to my mother. John came to dinner last night with them and we had a good time. Ryan became a little too much for John to handle but…

Ryan's top front teeth are very loose—they may be gone for Christmas.

SEXUALITY AND SEPARATED PARENTS

What did I know of sexuality? Very little. I wasn't clueless when it came to the emotional need that relationships fulfilled, but I was incredibly naïve when it came to sexuality. I remember my father taking me to an art studio where one of his friends was working on a series of paintings that had naked men and women running hand in hand through the cosmic reaches of space. I found these images to be bizarre, silly, and destined to be on the covers of paperback books in the grocer's checkout isle. I didn't see them as something I should blush at.

Did I know my father and mother were both dating men? Yes, but I had yet to learn that there were words to define them or that the world believed that there was anything inherently good or bad based on these preferences. It was a simple truth and I didn't struggle with it. I wouldn't have directly associated my parent's divorce with my father's interest in men. For as smart as I was, that would have been beyond my comprehension.

I had simply never known my parents when they had lived together. Their being apart felt natural. I wasn't ambivalent when it came to who my parents dated. Charming didn't appreciate Mom and I resented him for the sadness he gave her. I liked having Bryan around. He was welcome in the little world my father and I shared. I wasn't there to witness all the nuances of their relationship in the way that I was with Mom and Charming, but Bryan appeared to make my father happy and he didn't treat me as a character he'd like to see written out of his story. That made him alright with me.

INNOCENCE DISTRACTED

There was a family that lived a few houses down the street from us that had a son a few years older than me. He had a fair amount of *Star Wars* toys, a lot of which I didn't have and was therefore impressed by. He gave me a little pink ballerina. She was flat, made of plastic, and hardly scandalous but he had convinced me that it was something my mother wouldn't want me to have. I kept her under my pillow and would fall asleep clutching her in my hand. For weeks, Mom knew about her, but never said anything. Her curiosity won her over and she asked me about her. I was upset that she knew, embarrassed that I had been unable to hide her. She had been my secret, special friend. Mom knew I was attached, but thought it would be better if she took her from me and kept her in her sewing machine cabinet. I never saw her again.

BITTER SWEET

After I stopped attending Murray Day School on days when my mother worked, I was watched by Judy, a woman who attended our church and lived relatively close by (just beyond the cemetery and down the dirty slope), who had more than a handful of children. One of the boys was my age, but a year behind in school because the trend was to start boys a year later in hopes that they might grow big and excel in athletics later on.

In many ways, there is little to remember from these days because there was hardly any notable variation. Every morning was exactly like the one before: I would lie down on a couch in the front room for an hour or so before the other children crawled from their beds to the sounds of "The Candyman" song from *Willy Wonka and the Chocolate Factory*.

Breakfast would follow, which meant grapefruit. I don't believe I had discovered the trick of smothering the tartness with brown sugar, or maybe there wasn't any sugar to smother it in. Either way, I've never quite mastered a love for grapefruit.

Then, we'd walk three or so blocks to school. It was cold, bitter cold. My breath ascending as a white mist. Leaving school always seemed a bit warmer, even when the snowdrifts were taller than I was. It wasn't that I didn't like school; I enjoyed the opportunity of being around people.

Beyond Judy's living room and kitchen, most of my time was spent across from their house in a large field shaded by large trees that had drooping branches that extended far from the trunks, creating canopies and tents, blocking off the outside world completely. The leaves were green-grey, soft and velvety.

Under those massive trees, we would play the typical childhood adventures of heroes and villains. It was also under those trees that one of the others found a large brown paper bag filled with someone's discarded Playboy collection. Frankly, I don't remember it being all that explicit, nor do I remember really understanding what exactly I was looking at. I already knew that men were different than women. I had, after all, grown up in a neighborhood that was constantly populated with girls who were distinctly different from the boys in behavior alone. I had played the whole "show me yours and I'll show you mine" game, but was clueless to the process of sex and really had no distinct interest in it as such. The magazines, however, did draw my attention. I was aware that this was something I wasn't supposed to be looking at; perhaps it was instinctual or something in the other boys' nervous excitement. This wasn't innocent or safe; it was a threat and I wasn't sure why. All I knew was that it had taken things a step further from the older boys looking through the women's underwear section of JC Penny catalogues, which they often did. Driven by curiosity and undoubtedly the desire to fit in with the others, I ripped out a couple pages and smuggled them home. I hid them in a large twisted bush that grew against the fence in the backyard before moving them to my pillowcase. Within days, the adult world had been alerted to the newfound purpose for our daily jaunts into the netherworld and the magazines were, for the most part, taken away. For unexplainable reasons, the adult figure assigned to destroying the contraband randomly tossed a few of the magazines out into the empty field toward the dairy, rather than properly disposing all of them. Maybe it was a test. If so, we inevitably failed as these magazines were recovered by the other boys in the coming days, prolonging the affair. Soon after, they disappeared entirely and life tried to return to pirates and spaceships.

EMAIL EXCERPT: A MOTHER'S POINT OF VIEW

One day after I picked you up from Judy's I saw you take something from your backpack and shove it into the bottom of the wastebasket in the kitchen. You were not a sneaky kid and you were acting very strange. Later I went to the wastebasket and fished out the pages. They were some really raunchy pornography. I was shocked. My first thought was one of your dad's friends had given it to you. I remember going to my room and praying and knowing that I did not know how to handle this and wishing that you had a father in the house. I asked you where you got the pictures. At first you did not want to tell me but finally you told me that you had gotten it from some older boys at Judy's. We talked about it and you agreed that this was not good and that you would stay away from the boys. I talked to Judy the next day and she assured me that she had no idea where they got the pictures or that they had the pictures. A few days later we were in Smith's and you started acting suspicious again. I watched as you snuck [a crumbled piece of paper] out of your pocket and stuffed it into the produce (I think apples) at the store. I went over and retrieved it. You could tell by the look in my eye how disappointed and sad it all made me and I could tell that you were bothered by the whole situation. We went home from the store and talked again about it. There were several times when I remember just bowing my head and saying I don't know how to handle this situation but I know that it is so important how I handle this – help me.

LEADER OF THE BAND

My mother has been hovering over the Yellow Pages all afternoon. The theme for her and Kathy's next group date has them picking out musical instruments. Kathy is off tracking down a drum set (I believe she ended up with a Muppets-themed set with a picture of Animal on the kick drum, but it could be that in my mind, all drums were associated with the Muppets). Mom is searching for a conductor's baton. As far as I'm concerned, she's wasting her time. I'd tell her this but I'd rather not be fined.

So, we drive a seemingly endless distance. I'm bitter whenever we go on one of these escapades. Mom will put in hours of work and Charming will shrug it off like he deserves better. I'd say what he deserves but, again, I'd rather not be fined. Mom jumps out of the car and runs into the music store and returns with a lovely white stick with a brown handle.

I know it's important to her that the night goes well and deep inside I'd like the same. I snap the end of the baton off. I don't know how it happens, but these things always seem to. I didn't do it on purpose. It doesn't matter. She panics and is upset. Luckily, it's not completely ruined. She'll pencil sharpen the broken end and paint the tip white.

I felt horrible.

Still, of all instruments in the world my mother could have chosen for Charming, she picked a baton. Give him anything else and he's guaranteed to talk his way out of playing it. Give him a stick and convince him he's in control and he might just participate.

DECEMBER 19, 1982

Ryan and I have been busy getting ready for Christmas. We have everything bought, made and wrapped. Ryan sang in the Christmas program—good kid—and we went to the bishop's open house this afternoon.

Ryan spent the night and Saturday with Kathy in Ogden. They saw the fantasy park, rode horses, played with Kathy's nephews, went shopping and had a real good time.

UNRECORDED

There is no mention in my mother's journal about the role she continued to play in my father's life. She's never spoken about it at all. Kathy recounts the nights when my father, heartbroken and tear-laden, would come to my mother in the wake of another failed relationship in search of comfort and reassurance.

When I ask Mom about this, she shrugs it off and suggests that Kathy either remembers more than she does or that Kathy remembers her being better to him than she actually was. I don't think he had anyone else to turn to. His family, at best, tolerated him and would have likely presented him with a religious diatribe long before they offered sympathy. Mom was simply too kind to not be sympathetic. If my father needed a shoulder to cry on, she would have offered it.

I have no memories of my father being at my mother's house. There are scratches of images of him lingering at birthday parties, but those are stolen from my mother's recollections and not my own memories. Kathy tells me that my father would often spend Sunday dinner with us, cooking at his condominium and bringing over the meal or cooking in my mother's kitchen. I can't picture this. I want to because it suggests that there might have been some semblance of love and normality between my parents. They loved me and somehow that meant they loved each other as well. Maybe, in the end, I would have been worthy to be called Jason. I need to believe that we brought him a little peace and a morsel of joy.

1983

JANUARY 2, 1983

Another year—more resolutions. Some are becoming habitual. Top priority this as last year and previous is resolving this relationship with John. Next continuing my piano lessons. Third is being happier with myself and finding where I'm going; if anywhere.

Ryan and I went to Casper for Christmas. There was a record breaking snow storm and our flight home was delayed for 1½ days and I missed an extra day of work. I talked to John twice while I was home in Casper.

Ryan lost (actually I pulled) one of his front teeth on Christmas Eve day.

PLAYING PIANO

Mom did everything she could to make life a series of events and games. Practicing piano was not only an attempt to further her skill but it was also a way of entertaining my ravenous imagination. While she played her assigned songs, I would run about wildly, engaged in modern dance infused with a child's natural adrenaline. There was a particular song about a train that sent me into hyper hysterics. It pounded along at a quick pace with its *cha-chung* tune. I'd shake the house as I ran an oval through the living room, often crashing into a tired heap at the song's end. From time to time, the songs would disintegrate into the basic attack theme from the movie Jaws, which sent me running for the safety of the upper bunk of my bed. I would, of course, return to dancing when the songs moved back into happier melodies.

JANUARY 16, 1983

Since Christmas I have kept very busy. My piano lessons are going well, it seems I always need to practice. I have a new position as in-service teacher in Primary. I had my first lesson last Wednesday; it went fairly well. I've worked a lot—too much.

My relationship with John has put some pressure on me. It is very hard feeling as I do about him and not being loved in return. I know he cares but at times I lose patience. The relationship is good and it's worth waiting for.

Ryan is really doing well. I'm a little worried about how he is doing in his reading at school. His math seems very good but sometimes his reading papers could use improvement. When I go over them with him he seems to understand. He is a very good boy at school and Primary. He also is very fond of John and is anxious to have a "father that lives in our house."

Ryan spends a lot of his time pretending with his Star Wars characters. He plays well by himself and also loves to play with others. He likes jokes, especially knock-knock jokes. He likes to play "war" with playing cards and loves to make presents. I provided him with scissors, paste, colored paper, markers, stickers etc. and he enjoys himself. He is a good kid and I love him a lot.

JASON

How exactly Jason and I became friends is long since forgotten. I probably stood next to him in line or sat next to him sometime during the first week of first grade and in the wonderful workings of childhood, that made us best friends. After all, first grade is a lot like prison; you feel exposed and in danger so you quickly find someone who'll watch your back as long as you watch theirs. Jason was also friends with a boy named Josh, one of the popular kids, which made my friendship with Jason all the safer. I could blissfully believe I too was popular, even if it were simply by association.

I don't remember a lot about Jason's family; he had a few siblings and his parents were still together. Their condominium was two floors and somewhat cramped for the number of people, but warm and inviting. I didn't spend much time there. They lived only a mile or so away but when you're six that might as well be Texas.

One afternoon, Jason called and asked if I wanted to go see the new James Bond film, *The Living Daylights*, with him and his family. I was so excited that he would think to invite me over all the other kids that he knew. Sure, it turned out that Josh hadn't been home and I wasn't his first option but this did nothing to dampen my spirits. I had never been invited by someone outside of my family to do anything. This did wonders for my confidence.

There were a few sleepovers at Jason's over the next three years. Typically, this involved Josh, me, and perhaps a substitution person here and there. We'd enjoy a few hours of riotous play until it got late and then we'd watch a movie or two (*The Thing from Another World* was my favorite; *The Pirate Movie* was less impressive) to stretch us into the early hours of morning before surrendering to sleep. You couldn't be the first because everyone was aware of all the tricks and gags that could be pulled on the first to drift into dreams. I don't remember ever actually pulling any pranks on the first person to fall asleep, but the threat was always there.

ERIC

When it came to abundant personality and scene-stealing, that was left to Eric. It seems like he came into the picture later than the rest, second or third grade, but my timeline from that period is blurred into one long chaotic swirl of events that all seem to be happening at the same time.

He was the class clown, but not in that obnoxious bratty way that you see in the movies. Well, he might have been exactly that, but from my angle he was a friend and that made his antics less bothersome than they would have been for adults and those outside of our circle. Eric's parents were divorced and he lived with his mom a couple blocks away. His father was a popular sports columnist for a local newspaper, which meant that Eric was more of an authority on sports than the rest of us. Oddly enough, he wasn't as keenly interested in sports as you might expect. It seemed more like something he needed to know; perhaps it was the one string that kept him tied to his father.

For Eric's birthday, we stayed at his father's home in Park City. Apparently, my mother was reluctant to let me go, but when she learned that Jason would be there, she trusted the judgment of his parents and allowed me to go. It seemed palatial with its multiple floors. There was a real tree inside that stretched up as the stairway led down to the basement. Not even Kathy had a tree growing in the middle of her house.

At times, I wanted to be Eric. I felt like we had a lot in common but for whatever reason we were so very different. I envied the way that he could captivate an audience. Everyone loves the guy who can make you laugh.

HOPSCOTCH

If there were one thing the world needed, it was more swings. No matter how quickly you ran from the classroom to the playground, the odds of finding an open swing were miniscule. Finding someone who was willing to give up their swing before recess was over proved even more elusive. For whatever reasons, the monkey bars didn't interest me; perhaps it was the broken arm that came every autumn. No, my attention, along with a handful of others that must have included Josh and Jason along with the rest of the gang, was turned to hopscotch. There were at least four or five grids painted on the blacktop which was convenient until winter came and covered them with a thick layer of ice, frosted off with another layer of snow. We became archeologists wielding small screwdrivers, engaged every recess in the excavation of one hopscotch. Our process was slowed by a number of factors: the relative lack of strength that our little arms could muster, the continual snow fall that would erase our progress on a daily basis, and limited outside recess due to the poor weather. When we finally succeeded in clearing the ice away, the victory wasn't in the chance to play hopscotch. It was in the completion of something we deemed difficult, if not impossible.

JANUARY 21, 1983

It is Friday night and Ryan is away at his dad's. This week was report card time again. I was worried about how he would do in reading—but his grades were all good except penmanship (he inherited that).

I've been taking piano lessons the last couple months. It's hard for these old stiff fingers but I'm really enjoying them and my teacher is very patient and has a good sense of humor.

KISS CHASE

Is there really a time in a young boy's life where girls are not only an enigma, but also undesirable? I've always been beguiled by them. I didn't know I wasn't supposed to be. Certainly, I saw it in juvenile literature and film but I also saw talking cats and mice that could ride motorcycles. I, of course, put up the pretense of cooties and whatnot to fit within the social structure of being a kid; I had to. I also knew that someday, like Eve, I would choose the apple over isolation. How could I not? It all seemed like a strange paradox; my mother, a girl grown into a woman, was the most loving and uplifting presence in my life. I knew that the girls who populated the desks that surrounded me in classrooms, bunched together in hallways, laughing as they swung through the playgrounds, could all become as loving and self-sacrificing as my mother.

I imagine that the paradox wasn't lost on many of the boys, who, although we could never admit it, had to wear our pretense as if it fit. The evidence is in the frequency with which we spent our recesses running at half speed, engaged in something known as "kissing tag." The girls, openly liberated from their closeted feelings for the boys, were the kissers and we, the charlatan-strong and disinterested boys, were the hunted.

The chase was only as good as the catch. It took skill to find the speed that masked your true intentions of getting caught without giving yourself away. There was nothing better than being pinned to the ground with a kiss planted on your cheek, even if you had to act as if you were terribly disgusted. Disgust and disguise were the only rules and if you broke them, you'd be ridiculed by the boys and the girls might be less game to give chase.

In war, there was no room for turncoats. You simply followed the leader (who, in this case, was the rather athletic Josh) or stand alone digging in the sand or dangling from the jungle bars because you certainly weren't going to be allowed on the swings or the frontlines of the kiss chase. Standing in opposition there was always Dara: chief of all things female. None of us liked her, although we all dreamt of spending the remainder of our existence sitting awkwardly close to her in a place just beyond the view of our friends. Rumor had it that her mother had been a *Playboy* Bunny and experience had given me a vague notion of what that meant: Dara's lineage was attractive. She had chosen Zack as her prince and the fact that he had taken to the role, like any of us would have liked to, made him the boyish equivalent of a leper. He'd taken a bit of the apple and he'd have to suffer the consequences.

One afternoon, I missed the chase; either I had wandered off into fancy or hadn't attended school that day. It had ended poorly—at the edge of the playground lay Dara, her dress flipped over her head while my brothers laughed like wolves. Who had done it?

Had I been there, would I have protested or laughed?

There was a scalding tongue lashing applied by our teacher, but it was unnecessary. Even at that age, you have a sense of when things have gone too far. The price? Innocence lost and the remainder of the kissing tag season canceled. Clearly, the rules of playing house were different than those of war.

JANUARY 30, 1983

Last Saturday on the way home from work my car started acting funny and then finally died in the ZCMI parking lot—blocking traffic—of course. After honking, swearing and dirty looks from many, a couple of men and a policeman helped me and showed me how to start the car manually pumping the choke. The policeman followed me home. So Monday it went to the shop. Now it works but marginally. Yesterday I was out looking at new cars.

My piano lesson didn't go well either—my fingernails were too long and my teacher was out of patience by the time for my lesson.

My mother called last night. She said she hadn't been able to sleep well all week worrying about me. She always knows when I have problems. She's worried about John and me and so am I. I haven't seen or heard from him in 2 weeks and I don't know what's going on. I'm depressed and discouraged over it.

A BIT OF FORESHADOW

I learned early on that dancers were the most exquisite creatures God ever created. They were also completely out of my league. I had crushes, several crushes. One started when a classmate danced for show and tell. I already had a passing infatuation, the performance just sealed the deal. It wasn't particularly good dancing—interpretive at best—nonetheless, it took some intrinsic talent to attempt gracefulness while all our classmates stared, even if I couldn't place it. I could try and convince you that it was the aesthetic, the way she moved was this or that. I think it was primal. I believe her name was Tiffany, but it could just as easily be Julie or Kate. Vanessa? I suppose it doesn't matter; the damage was done. Inescapable truth: dancers are inherently beautiful. Maybe that plastic ballerina that I hid underneath my pillow did have a lasting effect after all. So many dancers locked in cupboards, just out of my reach.

MARCH 3, 1983

I spent last month car shopping. I finally bought a Honda Accord 4-door. So far I am pleased. I've had it 3 days. I did not like the way I was treated by the dealership. Their attitude or the below blue book they gave me for my trade in. I came away feeling very low about myself and the deal I had made. But at least I can go back knowing I treated them fairly and owe them nothing.

My parents were over President's Day weekend. They stayed at our house and we had an enjoyable visit.

My mother will never understand John but she supports me in my decisions.

I sent John a valentine and he called me. I talked to him again last Sunday. He's getting his head together.

KAREN

There was a row of large, half-buried tires at the edge of the playground, probably from tractors and other large farm equipment, but preferably evidence of alien life, remnants of a crashed spaceship, or asteroids camouflaged and imbedded in the dirt a thousand years before. It was there, or at least it seemed to have been there, that I stepped out and took a bite of the apple. Not a sin, simply a desire for a new kind of affection. Her name was Karen. I don't know if I had watched her from afar or if the moment, her being there alone and nearby, stirred a feeling within me.

"You're cute," I said.

"So are you," she responded.

As far as we were concerned, this made us a couple and having watched my mother try to impress Charming, I had a good idea of what I was supposed to do next. I went home and told my mother I wanted to take Karen something. Every 1st of May to celebrate May Day, my mother would make cupcakes that looked like baskets filled with flowers (a little frosting and a fuzzy pipe cleaner as the handle) and deliver them to our neighborhood, regardless of how well we knew them. I thought that a plate filled with those kinds of cupcakes would be the perfect gift to surprise Karen with. Mom agreed.

So there I stood on Karen's porch, my mother at my side. To shake my nervousness, I played with the clumps of dirt in the planters. It was a brief, awkward moment between children and amused parents. I offered the cupcakes, she happily to accepted them and then it dawned on me: I didn't know what was supposed to happen next. Fortunately, the moment of silence that followed was brief as her mom inevitably started a conversation with my mom about how nice it was for me to bring the cupcakes while Karen beamed and I couldn't help but be happy that I didn't have a brother preparing a lifetime's worth of jokes while watching from the backseat of the car. Upon returning home, Mom insisted that I wash my hands, telling me that the dirt I had been playing with was most likely evidence that Karen had a pet cat.

I have no tales of sitting with her by a lake throwing stones, hanging out on tree branches, running wild through fields, or stillness with hands held tight together. These two moments are all I have of her. Whatever Karen and I had was lost as quickly as it was found.

MARCH 24, 1983

Almost two months have passed. I have seen a lot of John. Things are going well—but I don't trust that it will last. Kathy has become very anti-John. She is sure we will get married but I won't be happy. I took him an Easter basket. Had dinner for his birthday. I attended his lecture on melanoma and he "attended" Ryan's soccer game.

Ryan has really grown up. He is doing well in school. When John was here he was a very good boy and said a very nice prayer over supper.

My parents were here this last weekend to pick up Nanci from school. They got to see John for a few minutes on Friday. My mother thinks we should get married and move far away from Mike and families, for awhile anyway.

We all had a picnic in Murray Park last night.

Ryan's school had a dance festival last week. The first grade did the Do-Si-Do and the Pat-a-cake Polka. Ryan danced with a little blonde girl in a red dress (Tina). She was so cute and shorter than Ryan! Ryan really did well—I think he was even leading!

Ryan has been playing soccer. He really has improved. He is interested in the game and though he hangs back a little he sometimes kicks the ball.

THE SPORTING ELEMENT

Despite what might be considered a rather unconventional environment—the cocktail of religion and the still-closeted gay underworld—my interests as a kid were pretty normal. Beyond the assumed obsession with all things *Star Wars*, I filled up the empty corners of my life by playing various sports. I don't remember expressing a real interest in them. Undoubtedly, my mother, who had grown up in a house full of girls, looked to the path Uncle David took with my cousin Jeremy to sort out how to raise a little boy. It started with soccer. Well, it sort of started with soccer. I lacked focus, determination, and coordination. I made up for these deficiencies with a blanketed sense of disinterest. In my mind, I was a rather shy child, but the evidence in this case suggests the opposite, or at the very least it points out a penchant for taking the spotlight, even if the stage was rather unconventional. Seeing as

I couldn't kick the ball, I took to sleepwalking the soccer field, oblivious to the action as it went on around me. The parents were entertained, even if the coach was not.

Soccer would give way to baseball, which would be my most enduring athletic interest. It was literally years before I would get my first hit and I always seemed to be stuck out in left field but I did improve over the years. Eventually, I pitched a bit here and there, played some second base and proved to be a rather serviceable player who batted in the middle of the lineup. Still, I identify more with the little boy, stomach full of nervous ache and afraid I might hear my name as the coach announced the lineup, than the adjusted role player. I wanted to be successful and even if my abilities suggested stardom wasn't possible, I was bent on getting there. Partly, I wanted to give my mother something to be proud of, but even then, I knew that her opinion of me wasn't tied to my performance on the field.

Later, I also did a fair share of golfing. I owned my own clubs. There's a trophy or two somewhere. Not a participation prize; something earned.

I don't remember my father being involved at all. He might have come to a soccer match, I don't know. I'm not the least bit haunted by this detail. I never knew my father to be a sports fan. We never sat down to watch a football game or play catch. We never bonded in the wake of our favorite team losing. We didn't have a favorite team. It wasn't a part of the world we shared.

Sports, however, were important to my uncles David and Mike. While I won't say that a working knowledge and interest in athletics was essential to fit in at family events, it didn't hurt. I may not have had a father devoted to this team or that team, but my cousins did. I attended many of Jeremy's soccer games, although the memory of them is never of the game, but of the crowd all lined up together on the side, yelling undeterminable support. He was far better than I was.

David was a huge Brigham Young University football fan, so much so that he had a giant Y logo magnet that he would put on the side of their van when traveling to home games. I spent many weekends watching football either in person or gathered with cousins and uncles around a television.

Seeing as Utah didn't have any professional teams beyond the Utah Jazz, most of my favorite sports teams were determined by factors other than locale. Early on, I figured out that it was far more fun to cheer against my uncles' favorite teams. They liked BYU so I rooted for the school my father went to: arch-rival University of Utah. In professional basketball, these were the years of the Lakers and Celtic clashes. Mike was a Celtic fan, so clearly I had to root for the Lakers. Besides, there were milkshakes to be wagered. Even if the team wasn't tempting, the milkshake was, and that was enough to set aside my Utah Jazz fandom for a week or two. In contrast, my favorite baseball and football teams were determined by my friends. I took the Dodgers in baseball because of Jason, and in football the Raiders because of Eric having a photo of their punter on his wall (it didn't hurt that Los Angeles housed them both at the time and as such became my favorite everything). Seeing as the Raiders' primary rivalry was with Uncle Mike's beloved Broncos, that worked to my benefit as well.

MARCH 24, 1983 CONTINUED

Mike and I have not been getting along lately. John is a problem but money rates high as a catalyst.

Terri and Mike have moved back from Lovell, Wyoming. Their house is being built and they are living in an apartment.

Bruce and Cheryl announced they are expecting their first child. She is excited. Bruce is scared.

MICHAEL'S LAMENT

As my seventh birthday approached, my father informed Mom that he was intending on baptizing me when I turned eight. Mom was dumfounded. He reasoned that the Church had done nothing to suggest that he couldn't. Which, of course, was absolutely true. The Church found it easier to ignore or not believe that my father was gay because the paradox of being Mormon and gay applied not only to my father, but also to those who knew him. You couldn't possibly be both and yet, my father was. Those that had known my father for years, particularly those that knew him as a child, would be asked to reconcile the positive memories they had of him with the all negative things that they had been taught a gay man was. To condemn (or try to offer counsel to) the man who they remembered as the smiling boy in an oversized suit jacket was too much to ask.

Upset by my father's announcement, Mom went to her bishop who brushed her concern aside by telling her not to worry about it. How could she not worry about it? Not only did she have a year's worth of arguing about the subject to look forward to, she'd also have to find a way to explain to her son why his father wouldn't be allowed to baptize him.

I didn't know this aspect of the story until I read about it in Mom's journal. I don't remember my father ever sharing his desire to baptize me with me. If he did, it would have only seemed natural. Looking back, it is difficult to discern my father's motives. Was he simply trying to get a reaction out of my mother? Or testing the waters to see exactly how much she'd let him get away with? Did he hate the idea of another man baptizing his son? Or did he believe that the LDS Church was true?

ME AND JOSEPH

Following my starring role in the commercial with my father, the mythological agents didn't swoop in with promises of stardom. For me, there was no sense of disappointment. The magical world of television had been somewhat of a letdown. If it couldn't raise your popularity among your peers, fame clearly wasn't everything that it was cracked up to be. Nevertheless, when it was revealed at church that my class would be making a filmstrip reenactment of Joseph Smith's refusal as a young child to drink alcohol as an anesthetic before having surgery on his leg, I couldn't help but want to the role of Joseph Smith. I wasn't holding my breath though. My classmate Joseph was certain he had the inside track and we all had to admit that he was probably right. We were wrong.

I don't know why I was chosen. Maybe it was pity or love. It didn't matter because I had what I quietly wanted. Joseph was crushed, but I suspect that in time he got over it.

I went with my teacher to Wheeler Farm, a history lesson dropped in the middle of suburbia. I had been to the farm many times—somehow avoiding the frightening possibility that I'd be asked to milk a cow. But this time, venturing into the old house at the farm's center (a typically boring location, due to the fact that you couldn't touch anything) was going to be a drastically different adventure. I found myself resting on an antique bed, staring up at the ceiling. I wondered how long it had been since anyone slept there. Would it be a hundred years before another head hit the pillow?

I was undoubtedly brilliant, or at least as convincing as the medium allowed. Not that it mattered all that much; there wasn't a chime or a beep to usher in each new slide. Clearly, they didn't know how these things were done. Beyond this, I remember nothing more than a room full of shadows as light found its way from the vents on the side of the projector.

I had always liked Joseph Smith. I knew that Mom thought highly of him and I was increasingly interested in talking to ghosts, of God or otherwise. I connected with the stories that revealed Joseph to be a rambunctious young man. He and Jesus had been children; every other religious figure had been born with a beard and a cane.

DAY SWIMMING

It is a warm afternoon full of sunlight, but the basement apartment is cast in shadows. There is a box of chocolates sitting on a table and my father is by my side. I'm not particularly drawn to the chocolates; I know they taste like coffee and I've been taught that I'm not supposed to have coffee. Besides, I ate one the last time we visited and thought it tasted strange. I eat one anyway.

Outside, we're bathed in sunlight as my father's friend, who like the rest has no face in the memory, shows us his new dog. She's tiny, snow white, and full of vigor and bark. I laugh as she swims through the unkempt grass. Her head bobs up above the blades, her dark eyes wide, her tongue licking the air wildly as she gasps in a breath before dipping back down and disappearing into the grass. She bounds her way towards me, but distracted by her master's voice, she dives away.

LINGUISTICS

My mother raised me in such a way that vulgarity's shock value was lost on me. When Jason and the other boys in class whispered and laughed at the phrase "funky chicken" from a Michael Jackson song because they thought he was singing something other than "funky," I didn't understand. Even in the film *A Christmas Story*, it was years before I figured out what word really replaced "fudge" and warranted a mouth full of soap.

For a brief time, there were two boys who lived across the street from me. The first time I ever saw them, they offered me a pair of one finger salutes and burst into fits of laughter as they ran about their lawn, pausing every so often to extend the greeting one more time. Later, after things between us had become friendlier, they would recount the event and still the humor escaped me.

Outside of my first-grade classroom by the coat racks, the rebel of the class told me (and whoever he could sucker into the conversation) about how he repeatedly "flipped the bird" at someone, a truck driver or something. Flipped the bird? I didn't get it, but I was smart enough to say nothing. Instead, I strained to visualize the pint-sized delinquent throwing dead pigeons at a passing car.

MAY 22, 1983

This has been a good month. We've seen a lot of John. We went hiking in American Fork and Pleasant Grove Canyons last week (John, Ryan and I) and to dinner at McDonalds. Ryan had a great time, asked many times why John wouldn't marry me.

Ryan is doing very well in school, loves it. Really enjoys reading and math.

My mother is having a hard time emotionally. She is fighting hard. She will hardly leave home and she doesn't sleep at night. My father is doing everything he can. I hope it is just a matter of time.

Ryan has been really well; he has perfect attendance this year.

I've arranged for Ryan to go to a summer program this year at Small World. I hope he enjoys it.

BOUND & SMALL

Following the experiences at Judy's, my mother enrolled me at a daycare called Small World. It was here that I would learn of loneliness and fear. Much like in kindergarten, I wasn't quick to make friends; only in this case, there wasn't anything to distract me from the friendless hours.

It was a world where the popular, rather than well-behaved, were rewarded with king-sized Jolly Ranchers and I was quite aware that the odds of me ever getting one were a million to one. I wasn't the least bit popular; I drew no attention from anyone, not even from those who ran the facility. Still, every day when they would award the Jolly Rancher I would sit quietly, full of expectation. Maybe that day would be a special day when the unnoticeable were rewarded for their stillness.

Come midday, there would be nap time. While some of the other children weren't used to the practice, I was well trained. Naps had been a regular occurrence throughout my daycare experiences. At Murray Day School, the lights would go off, and those who couldn't or wouldn't sleep could listen quietly to the record player as it told various truncated children stories. At Small World, there would be no stories to listen to. Don't make a sound, don't move, don't do anything except be still or there would be no reward for you. I dreaded this time; the last thing I wanted was a quiet stillness in a place where I desperately needed to be distracted from the silence that encompassed me. I don't recall if nap time was to last an hour, maybe only a half, but I had figured out how to count to myself—one to sixty—until the minutes added up and the lights could come back on. On a particular day, the hierarchy let it be known that if anyone was caught talking during nap time, they wouldn't be allowed to attend the zoo with the rest of the children. I had no intention of attending the zoo; it fell on a day when I wouldn't be at daycare and I had absolutely no interest in missing a day spent with my mother. I lay still, counting to myself, looking forward as the years slowly moved on until I would wake as a man too old to care about Jolly Ranchers and the zoo and then, after eighteen hundred seconds, the lights came on. The Jolly Rancher was awarded; my name was read, not as a victor, but as one of those who would not be allowed to go to the zoo because of misbehavior. Not only was this a world that ignored me, it was a world that hated me.

This dislike for me was further emphasized when it came time for swimming lessons. My mother signed me up in hopes of me enjoying myself. I believe she knew of my tentativeness when it came to swimming, but wanted me to overcome my uneasiness. It was a fear that she herself hadn't outpaced.

We would board a bus and shuttle off to the swimming pool. The locker room smelled thick and heavy of chemicals. I could hardly breathe. It wasn't the water that I feared. I had convinced myself that I was unable to swim, that these lessons would only make me more of a fool in front of the other boys. I felt so awkward. I believed that if I should slip below the surface of the water this time, there would be no one who cared enough to pull me back out. Just the thought of the place filled my senses with chlorine; cold rising in my lungs, air rushing out as water flooded in. There, caught in the dampness without escape, I learned I couldn't outrun my fear.

I endured the inescapable tightness in my chest and humiliation of swimming like a panic-stricken dog (water kicked and punched into the air just to keep afloat) in hope that my mother would be pleased. I complained, but took her judgment as law and pressed on.

A day came when our instructor insisted that we learn to swim without using our feet. I couldn't do it. Without my legs I was incapable of staying afloat; I thought that my arms were not strong enough. So while the other boys managed, garnishing praise from the instructor, I kicked away in my disbelief.

It wasn't a secret that I didn't enjoy my time at the pool. While many of the others ran in to swimming lessons, I was the one to drag my feet. My lack of enthusiasm, if not my fears, would have been easily noted by the instructor. In a better world, there would have been pity. In this world, I was to be made an example of. The instructor tied my feet together and threw me into the deep end of the pool.

I may have flayed about for thirty years or thirty seconds. I breathed water, fear, and the anticipation of death. Pulled from the water, legs untied with the entire world looking on, I was told to go blow bubbles in the small pool with the little girls.

If this had only been a Disney film; I would have been thrown in the water and in my moment of panic found the inner strength to swim. If I only had held the belief that my webbed toes somehow symbolized that I was made for water, that I was designed to out-pace the finest of swimmers. If I only believed that I could do it. If my mother had been there to shout words of encouragement maybe I would have escaped my fears, instead of diving deeper into them.

It was during this time that my father went into the hospital.

1984

JUNE 3, 1984

More than a year has passed since my last entry. You might guess—one of the hardest periods of my life has passed—I hope. Another strength building time that was too painful to record but should have been—especially for Ryan.

Last summer Ryan's father had a nasal septum reconstruction done after suffering from sinus problems for months. It was done on an outpatient basis and he was home the same day. After the surgery he had a variety of health problems—infections, digestive problems etc. that seemed to wear him down. Ryan spent the weekend with him the end of July when I went to the Shakespearean Festival. When I returned Mike was noticeably weaker. The next two weeks he spent as much time with Ryan as he could but he was not well.

GRAFFITI

Bryan, my father, and I had gone on a hike in the mountains. Nothing too strenuous but it left my father winded and he could hardly make it down the mountain. I hadn't noticed. I wasn't watching him as closely as Bryan. It was summer and I had my own difficulties with the mountain terrain.

My father hadn't been feeling well a few months before either, when Mom had picked me up in January. She saw that his eyes were turning yellow and insisted that he see a doctor because it was clear that he had hepatitis B and his liver was failing. Over the next few months, Dad would visit various doctors about a string of seemingly unconnected aliments. I was clueless. Mom was unaware. Because he was seeing so many different doctors, no one suspected the unimaginable.

In the spring, Dad asked Mom some questions about cancer. Mom told him he didn't have cancer and to stop worrying about it. She had begun to think he was a hypochondriac and didn't take his panic too seriously.

I don't remember ever seeing my father sick, not until he was hospitalized. Maybe I hadn't been with him nearly as much as I normally would. He and Bryan had gone on a few vacations together and that left me staying with Jackie on some of the weekends my mother worked. Maybe life-threatening sicknesses and death were simply unfathomable.

The clock was unwinding and we were unaware. I suppose our naivety was a blessing in disguise. Even an early diagnosis would have come too late.

NOT TO BE

I had spent an extended weekend with my father while Mom and Kathy made their annual journey to the Utah Shakespearean Festival. Somehow, after two years of begging, Kathy had convinced Charming to come along. It was a wonderful handful of days for Mom. They all stayed in the dorms of the Southern Utah State College (now Southern Utah University) campus where the festival takes place, which, knowing her as I do, would have been playful rejuvenation. A welcomed return to the days before real disappointment existed.

While attending the elaborate Renaissance Feast, Charming was randomly chosen as royalty and he took to the role with more gusto than anyone could have imagined as he and Mom paraded about. All the effort, the years of heartache and hope, had finally paid off.

It was the journal entry she would never write.

Returning home, she found a dying ex-husband and soon after, a terrified son. Meanwhile in Wyoming, having found the cupboard bare of children, Grandma Beverly fell into a heavy depression and was hospitalized in the Psychiatric Ward in Casper. This detail was carefully hidden from her grandchildren.

During this era, Kathy would also beat my mother back to the altar. Her fiancé, Dean, had made a lot of money in the oil industry and lived a life that seemed very extravagant. Mom never seemed negative towards him. She disapproved of his social drinking; I don't think I was cognizant of that until much later. I don't know if Dean was religious, but his occasional beer on its own would have kept the marriage from taking place in an LDS Temple.

Kathy tells me that, when the day of the wedding arrived, my mother, though supportive in her own right, stood in Kathy's doorway, refusing to let Kathy leave and marry Dean. Mom was unsuccessful, but it was a defining moment that Kathy looks back on with a certain warmth saying, "Only a true friend would do that."

JUNE 3, 1984 CONTINUED

The weekend of August 13-14 my family was in town for a family re-union. Mike said he was under doctor's care and had been home resting up. Ryan usually spent Friday nights with his dad. Since my family was here Ryan stayed home. I thought it would give Mike a break. Mike called on

Sunday to talk to Ryan and to say that he needed to talk to me soon. He sounded scared and tired.

Mike called the next day (Monday, August 15) said he had not thought he would make it through the night. He told me where his important papers were and went over finances with me. He said he had asked his doctor to hospitalize him the night before but he had refused. He said he had an appointment that morning and he hoped his mother could take him. I offered to help if she couldn't. He said he wasn't going to make it and he was sorry for all the hurt he had caused.

I called Mike back awhile later and there was no answer. I knew his mother had taken him. Ryan made his dad a get-well card. It had his dad in a hospital and said get well.

After lunch we stopped by [Mike's condo] to give it to him. As we got to his door Mike and his mother were coming out. Mike had really deteriorated since I had seen him last. Extremely thin, face very gaunt and his breathing shallow and fast. Ryan ran to his dad and he turned away. Mike said, "Ryan doesn't want to see me like this." I hugged Mike and said Ryan loved him and it didn't matter what he looked like. Mike's mother said they were on the way to the hospital—LDS, where I work. We helped Mike down the stairs and to the car where he had oxygen waiting. On oxygen Mike breathed easier and his color improved. Mike explained to Ryan about the oxygen. [That morning] the doctor had found that Mike had pneumonia and he was an emergency admission.

Ryan and I went with them to the hospital. I got Mike admitted and they took him straight to his room (2E65). Dr. Dennis Kay wheeled him from admitting to his room.

DR. KAY

Although Dr. Kay was not my father's doctor during his hospital stays, he was particularly interested in my father's condition. Dr. Kay was a rare breed for the early '80s: an openly gay man. During this first stay, my mother felt like he went to great lengths to keep her out of the loop. Apparently, Dr. Kay had told others that she wasn't aware of my father's sexual orientation.

My mother had worked alongside Dr. Kay on a number of occasions doing bone marrow tests. She didn't know that he knew my father socially, but it wasn't any sort of shock.

She believes that Dr. Kay considered my father to belong more to the gay community than he did to her or me. That he thought it was in Mike's and his best interest to keep my mother as uninvolved as possible. I think Dr. Kay knew he was looking at Utah's first AIDS patient. He was terrified.

JUNE 3, 1984 CONTINUED

Backtracking—I had known this would happen for a long time. I had watched the disease progress—weight loss, fatigue, parasitic infection, fever etc. Pneumonia was the final symptom. My friend John had kept me up to date with the latest literature and I knew the facts. The previous January I had talked to a pathologist about the disease from an infectious standpoint. I had been concerned for Ryan—Dr. Laub had laughed and told me not to worry—but even then I knew.

FOR CERTAIN

AIDS seemed like such horror movie disease—no treatment, no hope, where did it come from, how did you get it—but it seemed very unreal that we would have to deal with it.

This was my mother's first reaction when Charming began supplying her with various articles from medical journals. They were few on facts, heavy on speculation. But the facts were never good; they were horrific. The media was quick to latch onto the more sensational elements of this newly discovered disease. Many felt that it was God's punishment to rid the world of gays and later, IV drug users were thrown into the mix. There was a lot of hysteria, genuine and merited fear. Still, San Francisco and New York City felt so far away from Salt Lake City.

Many of the doctors at LDS Hospital believed it unlikely that they would ever have to treat, let alone diagnose, anyone with this new disease. The majority hadn't read the medical journal articles.

But in 1982, a man who was traveling through Utah had to be hospitalized overnight. It was suspected that he had AIDS. Someone had hung a big, handmade sign in the lab, telling Mom and her co-workers to use extreme caution because the patient had an untreatable, fatal disease.

In January of 1983, my mother overheard one of the Blood Bank pathologists talking about AIDS and his concern about blood transfusions and the risks associated. Mom took him aside and asked him what the possibility was of my father contracting the disease. He told her not to worry, AIDS hadn't come to Utah and the risk of coming down with AIDS were about the same as contracting hepatitis. My father had hepatitis, she said. The doctor was a little shocked, but still told her not to worry about it.

But she had worried and now a diagnosis seemed inevitable.

JUNE 3, 1984 CONTINUED

That night Ryan called and talked to his dad. The next day I talked to Dr. Kay. I explained that though we were divorced I still cared and would do anything I could. I asked about Ryan visiting and received permission. I talked to Dr. Cannon in the lab and told him what I was sure Mike had—he was inclined to agree with me but would reserve judgment until the cause of the pneumonia was found. The doctors decided an open lung biopsy was too risky in his condition and were opting for sputum culture.

Ryan went to visit his dad in the hospital that night. Mike was in isolation so we had to gown up and wash well.

DR. CANNON

Dr. Cannon had been one of the few doctors who had read the medical journals and kept abreast of developments in the study of what was once considered the "Gay Cancer." He was one of the pathologists in the lab and a good friend of Charming's. While the majority of the hospital staff refused to even consider that my father had AIDS, he and my mother braced for the backlash.

WINDOWS

My father and yet not my father lay weak in his hospital bed. Trapped in a world too clinical to be comfortable, his eyes lulled as he gave in to the numbness. Looking out the window, my father explains that the card I had given him had been taken by the wind. A white square on an otherwise black roof two hundred feet below. We were hopeful—at least enough to think that cards could comfort away the hurt.

In my memories, my father was alone, distanced from the rest of the dying and healing. It was a twisting path that led past cubicles and janitor closets. It was at the other side of the world; the haunted wing of the hospital where no one dared to go. Those who arrived at my father's door were either lost or incredibly brave. I suppose I was a bit lost myself, perhaps a little brave. Put on the gloves, the mask, be careful how you breathe, the breath you steal could be his last. The gravity of the situation is clear, but surely he couldn't die. Not now, not here alone.

JUNE 3, 1984 CONTINUED

The sputum were unacceptable for diagnosis and Mike was getting no better so on Wednesday late afternoon they decided to do an open lung biopsy (LS Richards). I went down and took Mike's flowers from his room and took them to the lab. His mother was there. She was not too friendly. On the way home from the hospital on Monday she had begged me to re-marry Mike. She was convinced that he had changed. I told her I couldn't do it.

THE PAINTER CONTINGENT

There was the suggestion that my father's sexuality had aided to the disinte-gration of his parents' marriage. When he was admitted into the hospital, his parents had already separated and were somewhere in the process of tidying up a divorce. Gloria blamed Bob for not being a better father for Mike—ac-cusing him of being weak. Gloria, for her part, blamed herself for pushing my father away from his model girlfriend. She told my mother that if she had let Mike marry a different kind of girl, things would have turned out differently.

"I can't believe he overcame polio just to have this," she said.

Gloria felt that her time was best spent praying in the LDS Temple and would rarely visit the hospital.

Bob was hurt, attacked by his son's actions and his wife's accusations. All he ever wanted was to avoid confrontation. He was at the hospital every day and was a kind support to my mother.

Dawn, my father's oldest sister, was forbidden by her husband to visit the hospital. She contests that, insists that wasn't the case. Nonetheless, she never visited. My father's other siblings filtered in and out without making much of an impression. The awkwardness of his situation combined with being forced to take sides in their parents' separation was too much to face.

JUNE 3, 1984 CONTINUED

After surgery Mike was put into 4 South intensive care for "overnight." No one else was there when he came out of surgery so I went in to be with him for a few minutes. He was on a respirator but was soon able to go to mask oxygen.

Backtracking a little on Tuesday Bryan, Mike's friend, had called and asked me to have lunch with him—he was in Mike's room. We went to the cafeteria. He was very upset and scared. He assured me many times that the disease could not be what I thought it might be. That the doctors were barely considering it. That day the laboratory was informed of the suspected illness for precautionary measures. Later infectious disease people came to talk to the director who was concerned that I would obtain too much privileged information—Mike didn't want me to know what he had—something he never did admit directly to me. Dr. Cannon told them that I knew before they did and they learned to deal with me.

IT'S NOT 1982 ANYMORE

A little knowledge is a dangerous thing and that would describe what went on in the hospital.

The patient who had passed through the year before had simply been patched up and moved on. Not many of the hospital staff was involved. When my father arrived, he required doctors and nurses, phlebotomists to draw his blood, lab techs to handle his blood and urine, medical techs to test the blood and urine, respiratory therapists to do breathing treatments for his pneumonia, housekeeping staff, surgery techs to assist in surgery, and dialysis techs to dialyze his blood after his kidneys failed. The hospital tried to keep it as quiet as possible. Outside my father's room were big yellow signs warning that my father was infectious. My mother was even asked by a respiratory therapist, who assumed she was going in as a professional and not an ex-wife, if she knew why my father was in Infectious Isolation and Respiratory Isolation. What could he possibly have? She lied and said she didn't know. She then put on the mask, gloves, and paper gown to simply see my father. He was heavily drugged and out of it.

But news and rumor spread fast. One of the surgery techs had cut herself with something during surgery. One of the people who worked in the lab with my mother cut herself on a glass slide that had my father's urine on it and refused to do any more work on him.

When blood from my father came into the lab, my mother automatically did it. It wasn't long before she would hear them whispering in the halls, in line at the cafeteria, "She's the ex-wife of the guy with AIDS."

An IV drug user was soon diagnosed at the University of Utah Hospital. Salt Lake City's AIDS population had doubled in less than a week. It wasn't long before the media knew. Confidentiality laws were long from being in place. There was nothing the hospital could do, but beg for professional silence.

JUNE 3, 1984 CONTINUED

The next morning (Thursday) Mike was still in intensive care. They were having trouble with his blood pressure. He was in very strict isolation with no visitors. I approached the window—Mike recognized me and motioned me to come in. I found a g spirits were bad. I asked him if he would like to see Ryan. He said "Of course." I talked to the nurses, they thought I was crazy but gave permission. They cleaned Mike up and we waited about 45 minutes. Then I gowned Ryan up, put gloves and a mask on him and dressed the same way and went into Mike's room. Mike seemed glad to see Ryan and Ryan was glad to see him. The visit was short.

BASED ON A TRUE STORY

In the film *Superman Returns*, a beautiful young mother takes her child to visit his father in an isolated part of a hospital. Despite the valiant efforts of the nurses and doctors, the father's condition is untreatable by any conventional medical methods. There is nothing that can be done beyond waiting and hoping for miracles. But what is most cruel: to allow a child to hope or to tell him not to?

The first time I saw the film, the scene didn't touch me. When I saw it a second time, I sobbed incessantly. Not for the child, but for the mother and the impossibility of her situation—stoic and destroyed by her own inability to find comfort, let alone offer it to her son.

JUNE 3, 1984 CONTINUED

Mike spent the majority of the weekend in 4S and then was moved back to his room on 2E. I took his flowers back. The Bishop and Stake President paid him a visit. The Bishop was very much afraid of the situation and could never visit again. Mike took offense to the Stake President's visit. But the Stake President did visit him later.

Ryan visited his dad several times and talked to him every day and night. When I was at work I would see him several times a day. Mike and I had some good talks. He apologized for past mistakes and asked if I would remarry him. I told him I couldn't do that but I would do everything I could for him. Mike's pneumonia got better but his white cells and platelets began to drop. The antibiotic seemed to be making him aplastic (a condition where the bone marrow stops making cells). They had hoped to send him home on the Septra (an antibiotic) but it appeared they couldn't. They took him off the antibiotic and although he continued to run fevers they couldn't find the source of infection.

UNDIVIDED

Everything my father had been taught, perhaps even some things that he believed, told him that his soul and his hope for exaltation was lost. His connection to his family and those that he loved would be severed by death. He had tried to change. Tried to live up to expectation. But at the end, he had to concede he was not the man his parents had wanted him to be.

If my father were looking for absolution, it wasn't from God. A god worth loving, with infinite and perfect wisdom, would know the truth. He would know with an exact clarity how desperately my father had tried to fit within the mold. His parents, childhood friends, teachers, neighbors, mission president, bishops, and the rest clouded by their hopes and dreams for Michael that didn't come true, would they ever know how hard he tried?

A man does not dream of dying with potential unfulfilled, a disappointment to those who should have loved him. What other choice did he have?

The presence of his father, my mother, Bryan, and other frequent visitors would have been a comfort; the absence of his mother would have weighed upon his mind.

I believe that my father loved his mother at least as much as he feared her. His desire to appease her was a vulnerability that he could never shake or shield.

When I met with Steve and Kay, my father's high school friends, we were gathered around my mother's kitchen table. We talked, looked through yearbooks for an hour, maybe less, when they asked me, "Did you know that your father loved you?"

It wasn't a statement of fact. Steve and Kay would not have known if my father did or did not love me. It was an honest query.

I never questioned my father's love for me. I may have not been the miracle that he wanted, but I was part of the one he was given.

In the panic of dying with all his truths exposed, did Michael know he was still loved? Not just in the passive, unconditional way, but as an active choice?

NURSERY TALES

I was introduced to the writing of British novelist and philosopher Colin Wilson through his involvement with the neo-classical band In the Nursery's 1992 album *Duality*. In 2001, the band released a limited run of Wilson's 1959 *The Age of Defeat* (originally retitled *The Stature of Man* for its initial American release) that included a CD-R of seven songs that Wilson recorded with the group. Being something of a completionist, I purchased it unaware that it would change my life.

The Age of Defeat explores Wilson's philosophy regarding the need for active, rather than passive, heroes. Heroism is not something that is bestowed; it is the decision to resist and reject pessimism and move forward in the face of defeatism.

As a seven-year-old boy, I wasn't asked to love or not love my father. Many of his co-workers and friends, however, were asked by society and culture to reevaluate the way they felt about him.

He was despised and rejected. He was loved, too.

When I had the opportunity to talk to two of my father's co-workers, Jeff and Judi Stokes, I asked them, if my father had somehow survived AIDS, would he have been able to keep his job? I was surprised to learn that my father's boss visited him in the hospital nearly every day.

In a contemporary setting, these visits might not be viewed as courageous. In 1983, choosing to emotionally support my father would have been viewed by many as a terminable offense in and of itself. To visit him numerous times a week was riotous.

By the time I was ten or eleven years old, when AIDS afforded preachers of all faiths the opportunity to dehumanize the gay community, my love for my father would be a guarded secret and a source of guilt.

When I turned twelve, I was required to have an annual one-on-one interview with my LDS bishop. I would be asked about my belief in God, the LDS Church, and my commitment to the law of chastity. I dreaded these interviews because I knew that there was one question that I could never answer honestly:

Do you support any group or person whose teachings oppose those accepted by The Church of Jesus Christ of Latter-day Saints?

I lied every time. I didn't just support a group or person whose teachings opposed those accepted by The Church of Jesus Christ of Latter-day Saints, I was that person. I had chosen to love my father. I refused to see him as broken and no matter how deeply I believed that I was right to do so, I always left the interview branded and burdened by my dishonesty. I betrayed someone I loved every time I sat down in that office. I just didn't know who.

NAMESAKE

In early summer of 1985, 117 parents and 50 teachers from Western Middle School in Russiaville, Indiana signed a petition to ban Ryan White from attending classes. In December, Ryan had been diagnosed with AIDS, having contracted HIV (which had been determined as the cause of AIDS in early

1984) from a tainted blood transfusion. He spent the next six months of his life, which were supposed to be his last, at home recovering from pneumonia and a partial-lung removal. In June, his strength returned and Ryan looked forward to returning to his classes that fall and resuming his paper route. Despite being assured by doctors that Ryan presented no threat to anyone around him, Superintendent James O. Smith determined Ryan would not be allowed to attend school that fall. Many customers on Ryan's paper route canceled their subscriptions, believing that AIDS could be transmitted via newsprint.

The following school year, the Indiana Department of Education repeatedly insisted on Ryan being admitted but school boards and judges continued to deny him. In February of 1986, Ryan was allowed to attend class. 151 of the 360 students remained home. Within days, Ryan was barred once more and a fundraiser was held in the school gymnasium, raising money to fuel the legal battle to keep him from returning.

In April, Ryan was readmitted. A group of families protested and started their own school. Ryan and his supporters were uniformly accused of being "homosexuals" and were subjected to verbal abuse and death threats. For the 1986-87 school year, Ryan was allowed to attend, but was required to eat with disposable utensils and use a separate bathroom and drinking fountain. Persecution was driven by tales of Ryan attempting to spread the disease by urinating on walls, spitting on food, and biting people. His locker and personal possessions were vandalized, often with obscenities and homophobic phrases. Ryan's mother was accused of being unfit as she struggled to provide for Ryan and his sister Andrea. That summer, following a bullet being fired through their living room window, the Whites moved to Cicero, Indiana.

In the fall of 1987, Hamilton Heights High School welcomed Ryan, literally with open arms and handshakes, to attend classes.

On April 8, 1990, Ryan died.

I remember following his story through the many news reports and a made-for-television film. I was more taken by the celebrity than the human aspect. I didn't see our connection, our similarities. Over the years I, like many others, would reference him, along with Rock Hudson and Magic Johnson, as those who changed the face of AIDS. Of the three, Ryan was the worst treated and the most innocent.

RATIONALITY IN A TIME OF MEEKNESS

"Don't have him tested," was the advice as eyes refocused from the father to the son. Summer was ending, fall and a return to public classrooms was looming. My life was destined to change, but how much? Would they needle me until my blood revealed its secrets? Even if the tests came back negative, it offered no promises. AIDS could be sleeping, undetectable until the unknown variable woke it. If I tested positive, the implications were extreme.

Would I be allowed to return to class? I had already spent the summer tied up in daycare. If AIDS were spread by casual contact, public restrooms, swimming pools and hot tubs, it was too late for quarantines.

My mother arranged that I be taken care of by Norma Maynes, the wife of our mailman. She lived only a few houses away from Judy, where I had spent the previous year. I needed love more than supervision and Norma was more than adequately equipped for the task. It was like spending time with your grandmother. Besides, they had an Atari and I could play games in the morning. It was decidedly better routine than grapefruit and "The Candy Man."

JUNE 3, 1984 CONTINUED

On Saturday, August 27 Ryan and I went to a sample sale across the street. Ryan picked out 2 stuffed animals, a raccoon for himself and a gorilla for his dad. On Sunday we took them to Mike. He had been moved to 7W15, a bigger nice room.

Ryan gave his dad the gorilla but then couldn't part with it so his dad told him to keep it and to think of him whenever he saw it. Ryan was beginning to come down with a cold that night.

GIVEN IN TIME

I have no idea what ever happened to my stuffed raccoon. The gorilla, dressed in soft white hair with a hard-plastic face and a thumb that could be stuck into its mouth, was unnamed but always referred to as Dad. I slept with him for years; even as a teenager, if the gorilla wasn't asleep next to me, he was within reach on my windowsill.

I can't explain exactly why I didn't leave the gorilla with my father. I like to believe that it has something to do with *The Velveteen Rabbit*. I may have already read the book, or I might have found it later and assimilated its story into my own. Either way, Williams' story of a young boy who becomes very ill with scarlet fever and is forced to give up his favorite toy, a stuffed velveteen rabbit, because it may be contaminated by his illness, feels entwined with my inability to leave the gorilla behind.

In the book, the stuffed-velvet toy is saved at the last moment when a fairy transforms him into a living rabbit. My faith in magic and miracles was waning.

I didn't expect my father to die.

No one was assuring me he would recover.

JUNE 3, 1984 CONTINUED

Mike's fever went down and they released him from the hospital on Tuesday after 15 days. He said he was never coming back. He hated it.

He had been so hard on the nurses that I was a bit embarrassed.

Ryan had a cold so we didn't go visit Mike at home. We talked and he sounded good. He went to the doctor on Friday and was well. On Sunday we talked to him and he sounded bad. He wanted me to draw his blood and run it the next day at work.

Ryan and I went over. Mike looked awful; he needed oxygen. I told Bryan we needed to get him to the hospital, but Mike refused. We put a call in to Dr. Reynolds. He called back and Mike convinced him he was not too bad. Dr. Reynolds insisted on seeing him the next morning in the emergency room.

The next morning Dr. Reynolds took one look at Mike and admitted him. I called the ER to see if he was admitted. Not knowing who I was, they told me that compared with how sick he was now, he had not been ill before. After lunch I went to see him in 7W14. Dr. Reynolds was very concerned but insisted that all was under control. I went back to see him that night before I went home. He was busy with the respiratory therapist who was doing percussion on his back. He hated being in the hospital; he hated his oxygen.

PROCESSION

During his second admission, the housekeepers refused to take the garbage away, so it piled up in the hall. Only a handful of nurses tended to my father. It wasn't exactly clear if no one else would do it or if the hospital was trying to minimize exposure.

JUNE 3, 1984 CONTINUED

This was Labor Day and Ryan had been fishing and caught his first fish. We took it home along with one someone else had caught to cook them for dinner. By the time they were done neither of us could eat them.

FISH TALES

The majority of my pets had been fish. I hadn't been allowed anything furrier than a hamster and they always seemed to escape their cages. Sometimes you'd find them; often, you never saw them again. Lizards were worse with their pull-away tails.

So, while the fish was cooking, I carried on a conversation with the lifeless creature. I had been responsible for its death and I while I can't claim any feelings of guilt or remorse, I know that I would have rather watched the fish swim wild and free through the minor rapids of shallow rivers, tail swaying and eyes wide. I pretty much gave up on eating fish ever again.

That night, I found a sleeping bag and set up residence next to my mother's bed.

JUNE 3, 1984 CONTINUED

Just after midnight the phone rang. It was Bryan, Mike had gone very bad and was in 5B—respiratory intensive care. I talked to Dr. Reynolds; they thought they had him stabilized. It had been touch and go. Decision: Do I become an insider?

I called my sister Terri, she came over and I went to the hospital. I talked to the doctors, they were intubating Mike (putting a tube down through his throat and into his lungs so he can be hooked up to a respirator). He would be on a respirator. They were putting in arterial lines to monitor him. A while later we were allowed in to see him. He tried to talk—he wanted a popsicle. He couldn't speak but could write a bit, though shaky. Bryan and I tried to calm him, I told him to get some rest and we would see him in the morning. That was the last real communication he could achieve. I went up to the lab and did a run of Urinanalysis (routine urine testing). Then returned back to see Mike about 4am on my way home. They said he seemed stable.

The rest of the day, Tuesday, September 6, he seemed fairly stable though less responsive.

EMAIL EXCERPT: MIKE'S LAMENT II

A few days before your dad died the Stake President came to the ICU where your dad was. I talked to him in the waiting room. He told me how sorry he was for you and I. Then we both gowned up and went in to see your dad. He told your dad that the church had let him down and that the time was past when something could be done on this earth. I don't remember him giving him a blessing but it was a blessing.

JUNE 3, 1984 CONTINUED

The next morning I received a call at about 4 a.m. Mike had a pneumo-thorax (collapsed lung) and they were inserting a chest tube to remedy it. I took Ryan to Terri's and headed for the hospital. When I arrived Mike was fairly stable but still in critical condition. The doctors wanted to try him in the iron lung to see if negative pressure would be better for him and maybe more comfortable. He seemed to want to talk so badly but couldn't. Off the respirator was no better. He did not have enough wind power to work his vocal cords and his mouth was so swollen by Candida (yeast infection) that you couldn't read his lips. It was very frustrating for him. I was down several times that morning and he seemed better. Then I received a call from 5B—I had better come down. Down I went. Mike had another collapsed lung; they had inserted another chest tube. They didn't expect him to pull through. I called Mike's mom; she was hesitant to come, but the doctor insisted. Mike's dad was in Provo, they would try to hold off surgery till he could arrive.

Mike had not been responsive to antibiotics and they felt that another lung biopsy would be necessary so that if he did make it they could treat him more intelligently. Dr. Richards was not available so Dr. Doty con-sented to the surgery. No surgery room was available so they would have to do it in 5B.

When I went into 5B (the intensive care for respiratory problems). Bryan was already there. Mike was in such critical condition they could not move him. He was on the narrow platform from inside the iron lung. At first I thought he was dead. His color was awful and his eyes were rolled. He was intubated [with] a tube down his throat to force him to breathe and his chest gave mechanical lurches. Bryan and I put our arms around each other and cried. I didn't see how he could make it. We each took a hand and held it and encouraged Mike. They felt they could wait no longer. We left the room. They spread a sterile field and began surgery.

About ½ hour later Mike's parents arrived and we started a long vigil. A doctor appeared about 4 p.m. and told us they were almost done. Mike was doing very poorly. They felt he would make it through the surgery but not through the night.

About 5 p.m. Mike's parents went in to see him. They came out, Mike's mother almost hysterical, and told us not to go in, that Mike looked too bad. Bryan and I went in. He looked very similar to before the surgery.

I called Terri—she went and picked up Ryan and took him to see Return of the Jedi, his favorite movie.

STAR WARS

At the end of Rian Johnson's *Star Wars: The Last Jedi,* there is a scene that features Temiri Blagg, a young boy abandoned by his parents in the gambling city of Canto Bight. To survive, Temiri lives in the stable and tends to the city's racehorse-like creatures, fathiers. On this particular evening, his friend, a fellow urchin, recounts the marvelous tale of Luke Skywalker's last stand against the First Order. The moment is interrupted by Bargwill Tomder, their foul four-armed taskmaster. Fleeing back into the stables, Temiri reaches out for a broom leaning against the wall and it moves telekinetically to his hand. He sweeps for a moment, before becoming distracted by the starry night. Staring at the heavens, the camera pulls back to reveal that he is wearing an antique ring with the symbol of the Rebel Alliance.

This scene perfectly embodies how I had come to feel about Star Wars. I housed a desperate need to believe that I too could walk Luke Skywalker's journey. That I could rise from a displaced youth through the inner darkness of desire and circumstance to become a Jedi Knight. Luke was seemingly insignificant, even to himself. Yet given the scope of time, he would become a pivotal character that changed the course of the history he lived within. Yes, the "Force" was just magical, a variation on the superhero mold, but in Luke's clumsy struggles to channel and fully use his abilities made it feel possible. Why couldn't such a power lie dormant within us all? I believed, like I believed in God and the connecting spirit binding the universe together.

When *Return of the Jedi* was primed for release in 1983, my fandom had progressed exponentially since the Grand Central incident. Nothing in the pop culture world was more anticipated. Before the film's release, I had been given the *Return of the Jedi* storybook. I flipped through its pages with regularity. Examining the details of each picture like a future blogger intent on finding the most elegant minutiae in the shadows. I struggled with reading, so I ignored the provided text entirely and made up my own interpretations based on the photos. I completely misread Jabba the Hut's character as a jovial John Falstaff reveling amongst the revelers. In an effort to win the favor of one of the girls in the neighborhood, I shared my revised synopsis. She wasn't impressed; she could probably read.

JUNE 3, 1984 CONTINUED

That night we took turns rubbing Mike's arms and legs and talking to him. Mike's brothers and sisters came to see him and left. Mike's blood pressure was very erratic and the respirator kept him going.

I listened to the machines all night long, alarmed with each alarm—waiting—wondering what I would tell Ryan and wondering if I should have given him the opportunity to say goodbye.

When morning came he was still alive. I talked to Dr. Black, a fellow and pediatrician—he said to bring Ryan. I went to Terri's and picked up Ryan and we went to the hospital. They were busy with Mike so we went to the cafeteria for breakfast. After breakfast we went to see Mike. They had fixed him up as [best] they could. We explained all the machines to Ryan and Mike seemed to recognize Ryan. Ryan told him that he loved him and I think that Mike cried.

Whenever I talked to Mike, and I talked whenever I was there, I told him Ryan loved him and that he knew his dad loved him and that Mike had been a good dad and that he was a good person.

Ryan asked questions about the machines and we showed him the iron lung (spaceship). Then I took Ryan back to school and talked to his teacher about the situation.

MY FATHER'S SPACESHIP

When they put my father in an iron lung there was a sudden upwelling of concern as to whether or not I should go and see him. In this case, it wasn't a medical concern as much as it was psychological. From a distance this seems odd, almost comical—at that point everything terrified me. My mother tried to explain it to me, suggesting that my father was in a spaceship that helped him to breathe. I liked the idea; often I had fallen to sleep imagining that my bed was a spaceship racing into dogfights and crash landing into dreams. Over the years, I would draw various versions of my spaceship depending upon the bed I was sleeping in. This would continue through my teens when I found myself bound to insomnia, which was more often than not.

Fantasy world aside, I started to sense that the end, despite all my tiny prayers and massive hopes, was looming. He wasn't getting better; he was getting worse.

He was only in the iron lung for a day so; when I went to visit him, he had left the spaceship. I remember waiting for what seemed like hours before I could go see him. Mom showed me some pictures of different iron lungs, none of which were the same as the one my father had been in, but I got the general idea. It wasn't nearly as I had pictured it; even now, my ideas of what an iron lung should look like put the steel reality to shame. In my world, they're given useless blinking lights and a structure more akin to Han Solo after he'd been dropped into the carbon freezing unit. To see my father like that would have been unquestionably traumatic.

JUNE 3, 1984 CONTINUED

The next week was a constant touch and go. His kidneys shut down, he went on dialysis. His lungs stopped functioning—bilirubin up. Blood pressure always dropping—dopamine up. Percentage of oxygen up and down. Fever up—hit him with antibiotics. Hematocrit (his red cell percentage—he is anemic) down—14 units of blood. Platelets down—many light packs of platelets. WBC (white blood cell count—high if infection is present) down—take off Septra (an antibiotic). Cultures all negative. They kept telling us not to lose hope. Changed the tube from nose to mouth because his tip of his nose was necrotic (dead tissue)—also his toes. Abdomen and all tissues full of air—actually gave him a more healthy look. Doesn't seem to be in pain. Eyes alert—answers some questions with nod—but has no [long term] memory—only short term.

On Wednesday September 14 they call us all together. Mike has Adult Respiratory Distress Syndrome—minimum time for recovery 18 months—his underlying disease maximum life span 12 months—probably less. We are fighting a losing battle. He is not responding. Are we prolonging his death rather than saving his life? We decide if his heart should stop we want no heroic efforts to save him.

Bryan is insistent—Are they doing all they can? They tell us they have probably done too much. They ask us to meet in 48 hours to reassess our decision.

By Friday Mike has improved. They are dialyzing (routing the blood through an external filtration system to remove waste products—mechanical kidneys) every day but his blood pressure is better. A little kidney function. They put him in the iron lung again. It doesn't last long. He is fighting it. They try him off the respirator—can breathe a little on own but tires very easily.

Saturday morning I take Ryan to Sparky's Fire Prevention Club movie. Then race to the hospital for a quick visit. Mike is running a temperature. They are changing the lines. I go in and watch Dr. Brown put in Swan Gantz (intravenous line so they could draw blood and inject, typically on the neck). They culture all the lines (later no growth). They feel he must have toxic shock but they can find no Staph (staphylococcus bacteria). He has the rash and peeling and the fever. Back on full gamut of antibiotics. They begin his dialysis. I go home to Ryan.

The next day, Sunday, I work. I check on him first thing in the morning as usual and then return to 5B at 10 for the daily report. He is not doing so well they feel we all need to meet the next morning at 10 to reassess the situation. I call Mike's dad. The doctors explain the situation to Mike as they have done before. He gets a scared, panicked look in his eyes. We have seen it many times before. Bryan asks if he would like to make a will, he nods yes. He asks Mike if he would like Evelyn (a lawyer Mike used to work with) to do it. Mike nods yes. Bryan calls Evelyn and we are led to *believe that she will come between 4 and 5 that evening. Bryan goes home to collect papers.*

Despite his medical problems Mike is very alert this afternoon. The doctors feel he could probably handle making a will. Bryan talks to me about the things Mike has mentioned to him that he wants him to have—the Mercedes and the condo at Spring Tree. I'm a bit surprised but would go along with whatever Mike wants.

Evelyn doesn't show up, Mike becomes less alert. The doctor says that we can go ahead with the will but if it is contested it would not stand up in court. I talk to Mike's dad—he is reluctant to give so much to Bryan but agrees not to contest the will if it is my wish.

Bryan calls Evelyn—she misunderstood—thought that we would call her with the information and she would come to the hospital after she had it typed up. So Bryan goes in—alone—to find out how Mike wants the will. He comes out and reports to Evelyn that almost everything will go to him, a little to Ryan. I am astonished but I say nothing. I know Mike's dad will contest the Will—it will be thrown out and Ryan will get everything. But I go home sick inside.

The next morning I arrive at work—I stop off at 5B. Bryan arrives at the same time. Mike's dad will be there at 8. The doctors greet Bryan and I—Mike is going fast. Call who we need to call. I call Mike's dad—he gets a hold of Mike's mom.

Mike's BUN (blood urea nitrogen) and potassium are extremely high. Mike is barely conscious. Bryan and I stand on each side holding his hand and talk. I tell him he's been a good father and Ryan knows he loves him. I tell him we would like him to stay but it's okay to go. We will be alright and we know what a hard struggle it has been. Mike is peacefully going. His father arrives and so does his brother Leslie. Bryan is a little anxious as Evelyn hasn't come.

A few minutes after 8 Evelyn arrives. The place becomes a beehive of activity. They start to stimulate Mike—he becomes quite alert. A pale frightened Evelyn reads the will. Mike shakes his head—he doesn't like it. She goes over it point by point. Mike makes changes. He does not want Bryan to have Spring Tree or the stock. For the will to be valid Mike must initial each change and sign his name to the will. A man who has not been able to hold a pencil for over a week. I hold the pen in his hand. Evelyn says even if he can just make a mark, but nothing. The doctor tells one of us to do it for him. Evelyn is horrified. Mike is going fast. The doctor orders Mannatol and Sodium Bicarbonate through his heparin lock. Thirty minutes later Mike is alert and initials the changes and signs his full name. But we have robbed him of his death.

They give him valium to calm him down. Evelyn leaves. Leslie leaves. Mike's dad, Bryan and I stay and pat and rub. The Mannitol and Sodium Bicarbonate are just temporary measures. We know death is coming.

LeeAnn, his nurse keeps us busy. Changing his sheets, washing his hair, brushing his teeth, changing dressings, suctioning.

About 11 things start to slow again. His blood pressure is down. His heart rate slows and weakens. By 11:30 there is nothing but mechanical breathing. Dr. Crapo asks if we are ready to turn off the respirators. He is finally at peace.

I put my arm around Bryan. Of the three of us he is the only one who didn't expect it and the only one it doesn't seem real to.

We make funeral plans, talk about cemeteries. I call the Bishop.

I go home and sit. The waiting is over. At 3:15 I go to the Maynes' where Ryan goes before and after school. I collect his things and tell them. Then I go and pick up Ryan. I wait outside his door. He comes out and I tell him I have something to tell him about his dad. His first guess is that he has come home. I say no and he says "He died, didn't he?" Then he added

"I knew he was going to die." He says he wants to tell his teacher. We walk back to the school and into his room. He tells Miss Dolton and she gives him a hug and says she is sorry. She asks if he will be at school the next day—he says yes and she says good because he still needs to learn. We go home and for the first time since his father's 2nd hospitalization Ryan sleeps in his own bed instead of a sleeping bag by my bed.

TRACING THE FIELD

My mother was standing there and I knew the world was changing. One step, followed by another and so on and so forth, I walked the lines burnt into the grass that outlined the soccer field. Was it warm? Was it cold? I don't know. It was bright, too bright for the words my mother spoke. Despite hope, against hope there was a resolution, an end to days spent wondering when this day would come. My father was dead and while it seemed to happen so quickly, it had taken forever. No more listening for the telephone at midnight, no more rushing to drop me off when Mom needed to be at the hospital, no wondering, no fear because the circle is complete and discarded. No more sleeping beside my mother's bed. My father will not wake me Saturday morning, ever again. Bit by bit, as he became weak and then weaker still, I could believe in miracle recovery but I did not expect it. Children are supposed to outlive their parents, but not so quickly.

I don't remember a word of what my mother said to me, all I can see is the boundary line burned into the field leading forward and small feet that already seem to sink a little deeper in the grass. We walk the entirety of the line, ending where we began.

Back inside the classroom, scissors, rulers and the sink with its swan neck, long and thin curving to its mouth. My teacher is petrified. Mom is speaking, I don't hear but I know exactly what is being said. Will I be in class tomorrow? Is that a voice asking from within or without? I had never considered not going to class, was it really an option? Best to keep going, don't slow down or you'll think too much. So of course, I will be there tomorrow and a thousand days extending from that moment to follow. Life in the wake must go on.

So strong that little man, full of hurt and confusion and still trying to be stoic like his mother. Unable to completely face the loss, unable to completely understand it while caught in the dizzying shock and devastation. How could life continue now? Why hasn't the earth stopped spinning? Breathe in, exhale, and again. There was nothing to worry about anymore, the worst had come and had taken my father away with it.

A sense of relief followed by a rush of fear.

In the cartoons no one ever died; the severity of the wound never mattered. Morning news, where the threat of nuclear destruction was all but assured, treated death with a detachment that offered no education to insulate me from the pain. Even Obi-Wan Kenobi's death at the hands of Darth Vader was softened by the Jedi Master's ability to speak to Luke from the great beyond.

My belief in an afterlife would have been acquired theory, not a self-discovered fact. Real or fabled fiction, I didn't expect my father to return as a flickering blue light or a comforting whisper of advice.

I wasn't prepared for his death, even if my father's repeated visits to the hospital signaled its inevitability. Death is a thought too large for thinking. What I didn't know was that I'd been sheltered from the fact that my father's body was rapidly disintegrating. His fingers, toes and nose were literally rotting from poor circulation. I only recently learned that as death loomed, Bryan was consulting with plastic surgeons, desperately holding to the idea that Michael could be made whole. What did Bryan see when he looked at my father's skeletal frame?

I tangled my fingers in Mom's hair; this storm could be weathered. We had no choice.

TREASON AND THE LIGHT FROM ABOVE

For most of my life, I believed that my father's death was an act of God's mercy. It offered a sense of absolution. To believe otherwise would put God on trial like the rabbis in Auschwitz who dared to hold their Creator accountable for the crimes committed in His name.

It's 2011, Kathy and I sit in a restaurant with fake leather booths and laminate tabletops. She listens as I trip over the rambling of words I've wrapped myself in. Disheveled and far too bold, I try to sound wise, but play the fool—an unweathered fisherman offering Poseidon a boat tour. When I suggest that my father's death was a blessing, she pulls the out carpet before I can dig a deeper hole.

"The cruelest thing your mother ever did was to be thankful for all the conflict she avoided because of your father's death. I would have liked to have seen him live to be very old," she says with soft-spoken conviction.

It's not so much a reprimand as it is an invitation. For twenty-something years, I watched the world with my father in mind and I saw struggle and pain. I didn't understand that I needed permission to feel angry so that I could learn love again.

Kathy granted me permission to consider a second narrative where my father lived, a place where all the things I wanted to share with him were not fits of fancy. To demand accountability needn't be treason; the sin would be to turn away without asking anything at all.

I had heard all the sermons, the damnable judgements and fiery rants. And while their arguments were unpersuasive, the repetition of their message exacted a toll. Eight years after my conversation with Kathy, I realize the guilt I felt for loving my father wasn't my guilt to feel at all. It belongs to those who insisted that my father is unworthy of that love.

A SIMPLE DEATH

I'm not sure how quickly the media were aware of my father's death, but it wasn't long. To the credit of LDS Hospital and its staff, my father's identity hadn't surfaced. The media, however, were aware of the date the AIDS patient had died. As a result, it was decided that my father's headstone would not have specific birth and death dates and the cause of death in the obituary would be extremely vague; its narrative would focus on his LDS background and never mention his divorce. Funeral plans were pushed together as quickly as possible. He died on Monday and they buried him on Wednesday.

I would wear a blue blazer my father had given me. Mom found some khaki pants and I would take up the role of little big man. My hair could use a little work but that's what father's hands were for.

I've never felt as small.

The sunlight comes through bubbled glass, leaving trails of light and dark across the thick industrial carpet. I don't know if this is the funeral or simply the way it makes me feel as I stand alone amongst the adults as they whirl about their world. Their bustle dances before me like the twice speed of a silent movie. It's all blurs and streaks of dull suit coats and subdued dresses moving in and out of shadow. They stand in clusters with scratching whispers. Some are here to comfort, others fulfilling their sense of obligation, and some aren't here at all. Occasionally, someone looks at me, says something; maybe it makes them feel better.

Traditionally, the funeral would have been held in a church building but my father's parents decided that it would be best for the service to take place in the mortuary. There was no viewing the night before; even dead, my father's body harbored questions and toxic possibilities that the State wasn't too keen on.

Despite all of this, the funeral is well attended. There are, however, three distinct groups: my mother's family, friends, and co-workers; my father's family; and my father's friends. Each hover in their quadrants, all awkwardly partaking of the numb, shock, and disbelief.

Had I been old enough, I might have sensed the tension and fear that was buried within the prevailing sadness.

Those faraway faces were contemplating the trajectory of my father's soul. Would he land in heaven or fall like Icarus into the vast unknown? The gay community was no doubt reeling. This was, after all, the "homosexual disease" and now it wasn't just in San Francisco or New York; it was sleeping in my father, waking in Bryan.

My father's body, immaculately carved with skin a marbled grey, lay in a casket—his soul elsewhere. Someone suggests I touch him. I'm terrified by the thought. I don't want to wake him. I don't want to remember him this way.

I know nothing of closure. I can barely distinguish between what is real and what is television. This is real. I know it.

In a large bright room, an unfamiliar man—who hadn't known my father since he was a boy—spoke. I don't remember a word of it. Neither does Mom who says he might as well have been talking about walking on the moon. The Mike he spoke of was someone she had never known.

My father's co-workers, Jeff and Judi Stokes, remember being offended. It wasn't a tribute; it was a condemnation.

For some, the process of moving on demanded they remember the potential of the boy and erase the actions of the man. For the rest of us, it was the sound of Charles Schulz's squawking adults.

NO COMMENT

My father's name never made the news. No one close to my father wanted to talk. Mom says Bryan gave a television interview hidden behind a curtain and offered up no names. I imagine it would have only taken a little private investigating to identify my father. Maybe his death made his identity less interesting. He has since become a marker on a timeline that has become so congested with names that only the end matters.

BRYAN

Bryan lived in a gated apartment complex that I drove past on a daily basis in my early twenties. I don't remember going there more than once or twice. I don't recall any furniture at all and while this may seem improbable, the truth is Bryan had so little. There was certainly a bed of sorts, a few shelves, and maybe a table, but that was it. Most of the apartments of my father's friends that I had visited were opulent. Bryan's was barren.

My father knew many people, but seemed to have only a few acquaintances that he could call friends. The one or two that I remember are shapeless, more an idea of a person being there than a physical presence; except for Bryan, he has a shape, even though I cannot recall his face. He was the only one who my father let into the sanctuary of the den; he was the only boyfriend I ever knew.

Mom says Bryan was from Pennsylvania and had studied to be an architect. He was doing some kind of apprenticeship at a firm in Salt Lake City. She thought he was nice.

Mom likes to bring up the night he and my father went to a party. I don't remember the circumstances but Bryan was dressed as a female nurse; my father wore nothing but a diaper. To be honest, it didn't strike me as all that unusual. I had been a menagerie of characters myself. This occasion and a time when my father took me hot tubbing with him (which I also didn't think was unusual), were often cited by my mother as examples of my father's occasional lack of judgment.

Bryan was diagnosed with AIDS soon after my father's second admission to the hospital. In watching my father's death, he would have seen his own. He also knew that without my father to help with his finances, he would be destitute. This explains the agonizing lengths he went to make sure a will was drawn up. I think he was shocked by how much my father loved me; it reveals a sense of the relationship he must have had with his own father.

I liked Bryan. At least until I was older and had been told the story about my father's final hours. For a moment, I tried to cast Bryan as a villain. Not because of the money, because he forced my father to die twice. Even then, I found it hard to hate him so I stopped trying. He was scared; we all were and each of us handled it differently. For his own sake, he couldn't abandon hope. My father's death surprised only him.

Bryan visited my mom in late November, two months after my father's death. Dr. Kay had taken him along to his family's Thanksgiving celebration. Watching Dr. Kay's family, Bryan realized how much he missed the interweaving relationships that a loving family offered. He understood what I had lost in my father's death. He appreciated how kind my mother had been to my father and to him. He asked if he could marry her and be the father to me that I needed. She thanked him, but turned down his proposal.

In 1991, Bryan died. Kathy returned to university when her marriage to Dean failed. She graduated top of her class. She, like my mother before her, entered the medical field. Kathy worked alongside Dr. Kristen Ries and Maggie Snyder at Holy Cross Hospital. She had been the one who had taken care of Bryan, had been a comfort in his lonely final months. He asked about Mom and me. I hope he found peace in knowing we survived. Kathy says he had suffered for a long time.

Bryan, hurt no more.

LONGEVITY

My fear of the dark was subsiding. In its place was something more terrifying. Curled up in a ball, my face against the wall and calling out for my mother, sobbing. My bewildered cousin Jeremy occupies the other half of the bed. It's just another weekend, generic in every detail. There's no reason to be upset. It's just a feeling that strikes without warning: once you lose one, you could lose two.

A COMPLICATED DISTANCE

Following my father's death, I lost contact with most of his family. I'd see Grandma Gloria, Grandpa Bob and his new wife Joy a couple of times a year. These meetings were arranged by my mother and she'd do most of the talking. With each passing year, the names of uncles, aunts, and cousins became increasingly disassociated from actual people. They were placeholders in a conversation I could no longer follow.

Starting when I was teenager, Gloria and I would occasionally meet for lunch. We only ever talked about me. Being a teenager, this never struck me as unusual.

The Gloria who exists within these pages is not a full representation of who she was to me. I may have been naïve but I didn't see her as controlling. I don't know how to exactly define our relationship. There was love but it was underscored by a sense of obligation. I was the bastard child of a different life, a timeline brought to a premature end.

I remember visiting her sometime in my twenties. She liked to make chocolates at Christmastime and on this occasion, one of my cousins was there helping her. Gloria had to explain who I was, that she had a son who died.

I tried not to take it personally. Gloria left Bob in May of 1982; the separation of their parents put my father's siblings in a situation where they were compelled to choose sides. My father's hospitalization and death a year later would have brought into focus aspects of his life that challenged their LDS beliefs.

Letting me slip through the cracks might not have been the right thing to do, but it is what most people would have done. I would have been a reminder of things that they would rather forget. I don't know that it was completely intentional. I was close and a moment later, I was a dot on the skyline, too difficult to reach.

I don't feel like I had a relationship with my grandfather. We weren't strangers but I can't remember him and me ever talking on our own, except for that one brief exchange when he gave me his life history.

Bob died in 2012 and Gloria followed in 2014. At their funerals there were faces to put to names; not everyone attended both.

Bob is buried next to my father. Joy sprinkles his headstone with Tootsie Rolls and brings flowers and wreaths for Bob and my dad.

LOVE WILL OUT

The absence of the Painter family would have been more difficult if those in my immediate vicinity hadn't loved me as fully. Kathy and Mom were at the forefront but they were hardly the only ones.

It might seem perfectly normal for an aunt and uncle to be willing to take in their nephew on weekends, but these were extraordinary times. 1983 was a different world. AIDS barely had a name. It was a terminal plague that dumbfounded a thousand years of science. Legitimate fears were subsidized with ignorance, religious self-righteousness, and social panic.

My father's sickness had nurses, doctors, and lab technicians refusing to go anywhere near him. There was no proof that I did or didn't have AIDS. Rumor was you could get it from public toilets. Were that true, imagine how easily someone could be infected if they shared utensils, airspace, beds, and bathwater.

Still, Jackie and David and Terri and Mike were willing to take me in when Mom worked. They ignored the white noise, listened to their hearts, and treated me as one of their own.

A few years ago, my cousin Jeremy made a comment that went something along the lines of: "You had to take baths last because you had that skin condition." I don't remember having a skin condition or being the last one to take a bath; if that were the case, it was done in such a way that it never stood out. For this and a thousand other reasons, I thank Jackie, David, Terri and Mike for loving me and my mother enough to take the risks that medical professionals refused. Thank you so much for looking past the speculation, trusting that God would provide safety for your children, and giving me a place to go when loneliness could have easily taken hold of my life.

It would have been miserable without your love.

ONE WOMAN'S LOVE

Miss Dolton, my schoolteacher at the time of my father's death, was hardly into her twenties. It wouldn't have been too difficult for her to imagine what my mother was going through. I don't know her personal history with death; perhaps she had lost someone close to her and knew how to address the pain. Maybe she was just compassionate enough to not pity me and loved me instead. She gave me the book *The Fall of Freddy the Leaf* and little gifts whenever there was a holiday. It is amazing what strength can come from being acknowledged, even for the briefest of moments, when the world is threatening to tumble upon you.

My work and grades didn't suffer but I became very quiet at school, distant and closed. Miss Dolton was concerned and arranged for me to be in Resource. She felt I needed some personal attention. I'm sure she would have given it herself had she been more able. I met with a volunteer, rather than a professional teacher or counselor, who would read with me and listen if I needed to talk. I didn't mind the escape and never felt like I was being singled out in a negative way.

DECLINE FOR BETTER

A week or so after my father's death, Mom's sister, Nanci, was getting married. Throughout August. Mom and her sisters Jackie and Terri had made several trips to Charming's parents' house where he still lived, to learn how to use a pleating machine to smock dresses for the wedding from Charming's sister Nancy. Charming was constantly hovering, his professional curiosity intrigued him with all things about my father's continual disintegration. By September, he had become affectionate and demanded Mom's attention as my world was ripped in half.

Mom, who welcomed Charming's compassion, asked him to attend Nanci's wedding and unfortunately, he agreed to make the drive up to Wyoming with us. In an act of appeasement, Mom asked if my cousin Jeremy could drive up in our car so I would have someone to play with. Tensions were already running high and the prospect of spending hours in a car with someone I loathed wasn't about to be balanced out by inserting my cousin into the equation.

Prior to Christmas 1982, Charming promised to buy me a Christmas present. Some ten months and a multitude of holidays later, he had yet to follow through and in his esteemed wisdom, he decided the tight quarters made for the perfect time to tease me about it. He said that my present was in the in the trunk and I could have it if I was good. Everyone, except maybe Jeremy, knew there was no present in the trunk. Nonetheless, I put in one of my better performances and Mom considered my behavior better than expected. Returning from Wyoming, Charming was given a speeding ticket. Arriving at his home, he began to complain to his mother about how miserable the trip was. He wanted to know why Jeremy was better behaved than I was. She said, "What does Jeremy have to lose?" I had just lost a father and was afraid of losing my mother as well. It was then that Charming started to talk to Mom about marriage.

My father's death had left Mom confused about what she wanted from life and rather than giving herself completely to a relationship with Charming, she focused on being a mother. To my disappointment, we still saw Charming quite a bit in the coming weeks. My behavior around him improved to the point that following a long day of sledding, Mom procured a "gift from Charming" from our car's trunk. It was a Star Wars cassette and read-along book. Something I would have actually wanted, but clearly not something Charming would have picked out. The act of kindness was so unbelievable that he didn't even bother to try and play along. His role in our life diminished. I think Mom was tired of making the effort. I know I was too tired to force myself between them.

A LIFE IN MOVING PICTURES

That Halloween, Mom made me a Luke Skywalker costume. It was the black outfit that Luke wears throughout *Return of the Jedi*, complete with one glove, boots, and a green lightsaber. For the neighborhood costume parade, we dressed up my bike to look like an X-wing Starfighter. I remember giddily riding up Rainforest Drive towards the early-evening sun. It was movie-scene perfect in every respect.

Later, we went to Terri and Mike's house. Their living room had a conversation pit that I decided looked like the Great Pit of Carkoon in the Dune Sea of Tatooine from *Return of the Jedi*. While there wasn't any physical evidence to suggest that a there was a Sarlacc creature sleeping beneath the brown carpet, I assure you there was one.

A year in the future, I would sit in the pit red-faced and happily embarrassed while watching *The Neverending Story*. I let slip that I had a crush on the Childlike Empress and would duck and hide whenever actress Tami Stronach was on screen. I saw a lot of myself in Bastian Balthazar Bux, the young boy who hid in the school attic to read a book. I didn't connect with Atreyu, the hero in the story.

There's also the story from this era of my life when all the cousins were left with a sitter at Mike and Terri's house. When the adults returned, they found us in the front yard, hosing down the cars with water from the garden hose. The scandalous aspect of the moment being the sitter was in one Terri's bathing suits. I remember the adults looking bewildered and a prevailing sense that we had been caught doing something. I wasn't sure what. I always felt bad about not using soap when washing the cars. I have no recollection of the sitter, the swimsuit, or how the situation came to be. I tend to remember the boring parts. If we had been a little bit older, it could have been a scene from a John Hughes film.

LET US LOVE

"Dan Reynolds of Imagine Dragons is putting together a music festival. Would you be interested in talking to him?"

Hearing from Jeremy, a local PR rep and friend I'd made by covering the FanX Salt Lake Comic Convention, often means I'm about to embark on some kind of adventure.

LOVELOUD was pitched to me as a day of music and conversation that hoped to start a dialogue of acceptance for LGBTQ+ youth in communities and families where there is a high rate of suicide. More simply, it was and is an effort to let these young people know that they are loved and that, regardless of what they'd been taught or gleaned from the world, they have value.

Being a member of one of the world's most popular bands and a member of the LDS Church, Dan Reynolds coming into town to announce an event that would celebrate LGBTQ+ youth was a major story. So much so that while I set up the interview, but we would have Holly Menino, one of our best reporters, asking the questions and putting together the package for television.

I was more comfortable playing a less visible role.

There is a place for anger, but I had seen others with the best of intentions go down that path and do more damage than good. I believed that if this festival wanted to be more than simply a day of music, it needed to be built on a platform of love and acceptance.

My endorsement of the festival would mean nothing in terms of ticket sales or lives saved. For my own peace of mind, I needed to sit down with Dan and see the event through his eyes.

Typically, this would have been impossible. There was no question that I'd get to meet him, but anything beyond a "hello" or "nice to meet you" was incredibly unlikely.

Life, sometimes, offers pleasant surprises.

Between the hurry-up and wait of television and a gap in his schedule, Dan spent an hour at the studio. We spent half of his visit in the lobby just talking. I shared my family's story. He told me about growing up LDS and how his wife and his friendship with Neon Trees vocalist Tyler Glenn had helped open his eyes to see the need for something like LOVELOUD. He wanted to amplify the efforts that were being made by people like Barb and Steve Young and Stephenie Larsen to shine a light on the issue of LGBTQ+ suicides in Utah.

When Dan left the studio that day, he had at least one more fan.

CHRISTMAS WITHOUT DAD

My father had always been the one to take me out to buy presents for Mom. It was one of the little and seemingly insignificant securities that, unbeknownst to me, had been buried with his body. As December approached, my understanding of the loss became clear and led to an entirely more frightening prospect. What if Dad had been Santa? I posed the question to my mother. Would I get anything for Christmas? She said, "We'll have to wait and see." She instantly realized the unintended cruelty in the response. I had already lost enough. How could she steal the joy of Christmas from me as well?

They say that the rewards of giving outweigh the joys of receiving and in a stroke of luck, my school decided to create a Christmas store where students could purchase presents for their parents. Not knowing what my mother could possibly want, I selected a tiny green lamp, like what you would find sitting on a nightstand in pre-electricity days. Mom had two electric lamps on either side of her bed that were in a similar style, so clearly this would be something she would like.

Come Christmas morning, I was relived and positively thrilled to find a tree surrounded with presents. That year's lot included the *G.I. Joe* boat I had so desperately wanted. Mom seemed pleased with my gift as well. Christmas without a father was different and difficult, but manageable.

LINGUISTICS II

The light from the hallway crept into the room. A shadow moved. The narrator of *Gulliver's Travels* stopped mid-sentence as Mom yanked the cassette from the boombox and spiked into the ground. I could hear it rattle as it skipped across the floor, ricocheting off the wall and going who knows where.

"Dang it, Ryan...!"

There were more words, but my mind didn't make it past the first three. It happened so quickly. I had already listened to Gulliver's abbreviated journey for two nights in a row and had complained. Mom was angry and there was this weight burning in my chest that hadn't been there the moment before. Maybe if I held extra still, I could disappear.

In my head it wasn't "dang it." It was something much worse. Something that Mom would never say and I was to blame for making it part of her active vocabulary.

Years later, I tried to lessen the burden and jokingly told my sisters about the time I made Mom swear.

"I did not," Mom growled through her teeth. "I did not say that." The more I suggest that she did the louder her denials became.

It became a running joke that would resurface when dinner conversation lulled. She'd passionately deny my claims and I'd push back just to get my sisters to nervously smile as the dramedy played out before them.

Mom doesn't talk like a sailor; she fights like one.

OUR CIRCLES CONVERGE

To a certain extent, the internet has been a wretched hive of scum and villainy since its inception. Between spam, phishing, and links that promise one thing and deliver another, we've all fallen down our share of rabbit holes.

When I started to write for In, a regional weekly entertainment magazine, in 2008, it became necessary for me to increase my social media presence. I've had mixed feelings about the entire enterprise ever since. I still manage to fly under the radar, a testament to my general social ineptitude, but every so often something interesting pops up in my inbox.

> *Hey Ryan, I hope all is well! I love seeing your interviews and adventures on my feed. Um, I have kind of a weird request...*

I've had close friends throughout my teens, twenties, and early thirties who knew my father died when I was young, but have no idea that he was gay.

Amanda Stoddard was one of those people.

Amanda had been a good friend to me in high school. We had run into each other a few times over the years since, as she embarked on a career in film and I ran in circles, never quite sure of what I was or where I was going.

We'd been friends on Facebook for as long as I could remember. Still, it was a surprise to see her name show up in my messages.

We are currently in post on a doc project on Kristen Ries and Maggie Snyder.

The legacy of Ries and Snyder is one of great kindness. Working out of Holy Cross Hospital in Salt Lake City, they provided care to those with AIDS in the late eighties and early nineties.

It was era that saw many AIDS patients abandoned and rejected by families and friends. These men and women were left to die alone in isolation, their unclaimed bodies disposed in unceremonial ways. Beyond the loneliness, the quality of care varied greatly for the patients who were chronically ill, unable to work, and didn't have insurance.

Ries, Snyder, and those who worked with them fostered an environment where love and dignity was as important as treatment. For some death came quickly, for others it was a long waltz made less lonely by the compassion of strangers.

Anyway, we interviewed Jim Debakis and he mentioned your father (it took me a while to figure it out) as the first Utah [AIDS] case, it's in the cut now, but I want to make sure it's ok with you.

My father's story pre-dates Ries and Snyder, but any documentary on the history of AIDS in Utah will inevitably lead to him.

We're are very close to finishing the film and I'd love to show you [it].

We'd meet several times over the next year as the film Quiet Heroes came together. Initially, they were using my father's obituary for a photo; I had them replace it with a solo shot of him from my parent's wedding. It's not my favorite picture, but I wanted to avoid using one that had Mom or me in it. I didn't want it to distract from the story that Amanda and her co-directors Jenny Mackenzie and Jared Ruga were trying to tell.

I wasn't surprised when the film was selected for inclusion in the Sundance Film Festival. I was jealous, but proud of my friend's accomplishment. I always thought that I'd be the one to introduce my father to the world.

I took Mom to the world premiere at the Rose Wagner Performing Arts Center. I had, apparently, not warned her about the use of the wedding photo.

I had viewed various versions of the film before; there was something uniquely strange about watching it with my mother in a sold-out theater. The story of me, Mom and Dad has been the subtext of my life. To have a piece of that narrative in a stranger's story is surreal.

I just wish it was a happier inclusion. I don't want my father to be remembered as a footnote. I've never asked to be the son of the first man in Utah to die because of AIDS. I just want to be Michael's son, Patti's son.

I went to the after-party alone. It seemed like the perfect opportunity to network and possibly find someone who had stories of my father that they could tell me.

I spent the night walking from one end of the venue to the other and then back again and again. I'd occasionally stop to talk to someone who recognized me, but mostly kept to myself. If there is anyone more awkward at parties, I've yet to meet them.

Quiet Heroes was picked up by Logo TV and won a Daytime Emmy. Over the years, I've learned that these stories about the early days of AIDS have a universal quality to them. We are all bound together by a frustration, fear, sadness, and hope that yesterday's tragedies will inspire tomorrow's compassion.

DOMINO EFFECT

In May, Charming appeared on our doorstep. A woman was claiming to be pregnant with his child and he wanted my mother's help. He was certain that she had set him up, but had bought a ring and got a wedding license just in case. Then, he disappeared as quickly as he arrived.

Mom assumed he had gotten married until he returned that night with a silk Chinese robe for her. The woman wasn't pregnant after all!

Charming's life spiraled out of control. In July, he called worried about the handful of prescription painkillers he had just ingested. Mom rushed him to the hospital where one of my father's doctors (probably questioning her taste in men) stabilized him. After a week in the psychiatric ward, Charming went with Mom to the Utah Shakespearean Festival but the magic was gone. He suffered from the backlash of withdrawal and worried what action the Medical Association would take against him.

ENDLESS SUMMER

That summer, rather than spending my days at Norma and Glen's house, Mom paid Norma's son Brent to take care of me while she worked on weekdays. He and I would spend our time at 7-Eleven, or downing cheap cheeseburgers before finding ourselves at the arcade where we'd surrender quarters to the electronic wizardry.

I had begun to discover music. It was the dawning of the age of music videos. My head was full of the images and sounds of the Thompson Twins, Talking Heads, and the Pointer Sisters. A Michael Jackson poster hung on my door and the *Thriller* video reigned supreme. Brent was more interested in the emerging metal world of Def Leppard but we could agree that Billy Idol was pretty cool.

Madonna seemed to be everywhere. I was drawn to elegance of her lace gloves counterbalanced by her can of spray paint and playfully enchanted by her blonde hair, which seemed exotic and a touch mischievous because, as my mother jokingly put it, Madonna didn't have "the proper color of hair."

It wouldn't be long before Cyndi Lauper established herself as the second coolest woman in the world. Her fiery demeanor and distinct individuality fascinated me. I vividly remember watching her on the television as she performed at the 1985 Grammy Awards. Her hair was ratted wild and outlandishly red with a bleached patch on the side that had been dyed like a checkerboard. I'm not sure that Mom considered this to be a "proper" color for hair, but as far as I was concerned, she looked wonderful.

In June, I turned eight years old and come July, I was baptized. With my father gone, the event lacked the drama that it might have had otherwise. I wanted my uncle Bruce to baptize me. For reasons that I cannot explain, he had become a favorite, perhaps in him I sensed a kindred soul, the sort that takes the roundabout path through life. Because Bruce didn't live in Utah, it was ultimately Grandpa Jack that baptized me.

THIRD GRADE

Third grade was one of the best years of my life. I was pulling away from the events of the year before. I suppose there was a part of me that knew what it was like to be an adult and it hadn't been nearly as much fun as I expected it to be.

Norma and her husband Glen were more than you could ever ask of daycare; they are beloved to me like family and their love was overwhelming (even when I ran through their glass front door).

At school, my classmates and I loved our teacher so much that for her birthday we arranged to be let into the school early so that we could decorate the classroom and prepare a little party for her with cake and drinks.

How we did this without tipping her off, I'll never be sure.

Jason's mom came to teach the class about drawing. She picked me out of the class and had me sit up front. On the chalkboard, she drew a detailed portrait of me. I was a rainbow of shades swirling about. I never knew I had so much color in me. The moment cost her nothing but time and a bit from her chalk collection. It only reinforced the idea that even in a world full of loss, there was kindness and that goodness didn't always come from someone who was obligated to give it. It was the thrill of a lifetime.

Not nearly as uplifting, but memorable nonetheless, was when Mom came and taught the class about urine. It was rather embarrassing. Fortunately, there was no class participation.

I played the leading man in the class play, a prince of some sort. Mind you, I wasn't actually cast as the prince. I just happened to know all the lines and stepped in when my classmate decided he was too sick to perform. Mom showed up expecting me to play a non-essential role and instead watched me run off with the princess.

My friend Eric would run into some trouble that year. It would seem that the powers that be were concerned about his growing dental practice after one or two patients emerged from recess with bleeding gums. Following a thorough investigation, it was determined that, in their opinion, a blunt pocketknife was not a suitable instrument to be sticking in classmates' mouths, even if he was doing so with their permission.

LEAVING NEVERLAND

In 2007, I received a phone call from Harv Hallas, tour manager for Black Rebel Motorcycle Club. I had met the band a few years before when they played at an event during the Sundance Film Festival. Paris Hilton and Nicole Richie were holding court in the club's balcony. Security wasn't interested in guarding the backstage area. My friend Maddy, who I had just met that night, went back to visit with the band. We mostly talked to each other, never stepping in the band's way. From that day forward, whenever the band came back through town, Maddy and I would bring them trinkets and soda.

The last time BRMC had been in town, Robert Been, the group's bassist, asked if I would be interested in coming out on tour to run their merch booth and serve as a liaison between the band and the fans who followed them from show to show. My life was at an impasse. It was time to try something new.

I didn't hear from them for a few weeks. I figured the ship had sailed and I was marooned on an island of my own creation.

And then, the phone rang. I had no idea what I was getting myself into.

Out in a world of strangers, I found myself telling stories well after midnight about Mom, Dad, and me. Without those conversations, I would have never been able to sit down and completely immerse myself in this story.

Following the tour, I resumed my role as an entertainment journalist on a full-time basis. In some of my articles, I began to explore my feelings for my father in a more public way.

I didn't think that there would be people who actually read what I wrote. And yet, there were times when I'd be approached by acquaintances and strangers who had stories that were similar to mine. There were members of the LDS faith who were struggling with the Church's policies and opinions regarding the gay community. They had friends, relatives, co-workers, and neighbors who were in same-sex relationships. They were taught to disapprove, but the idea that anyone should be chastised and ostracized felt contradictory to everything else they had ever been taught. They wanted to love and were looking to me for permission and reassurance.

I didn't set out to build a small sanctuary where it was okay to talk about ideas and feelings that people were afraid to discuss with their friends and family. I thought the writing was for myself. I wasn't trying to tell anyone what they should do. So, at some point in every one of these conversations, I would question my own beliefs. Was I doing the right thing?

I spoke very little; I listened a lot.

CHRISTMAS WITHOUT DAD II

The next year they did not have the Christmas store at the school. I thought about it a few days before Christmas but then pushed it to the back of my busy pre-Christmas mode. The morning of Christmas Ryan was upset that he did not have a present for me. I told him that we would go out and get me something at the Christmas sales. Ryan was still upset and could not be tricked into feeling better.

It was the worst Christmas in the history of the world. Well, it was mine.

Charming was still moving in and out of the picture. Mom was exactly what he needed. His family loved my mother. Mom's family wanted to see her happy and were enamored with his good looks and profession. The doctors at the hospital thought my mom would stabilize Charming and were very supportive of the idea that they marry. Charming continued to talk of a future they could spend together. She wanted to believe in it.

NEW YEAR'S CRASHING

For New Year's Eve, Dean and Kathy were hosting a party at Dean's posh club, the Petroleum. Mom and Charming went. Mom was fascinated by the glamour, feeling like she had stepped directly into a high-class New York speakeasy. White leather booths with high curving backs, a large bar, tables with white tablecloths, dim but sparkling lights around the bandstand, and a small dance floor. Swimming through the guests was a large ensemble of waiters to attend to your every need. They sat at Dean and Kathy's table, drawing a few curious glances—not just anyone would be sitting with the hosts. Mom felt out of place and detached from the action. Charming took to the scene with a swagger, until Dean announced that the Society writer for the newspaper was showing up to take some photos. Photos were taken, everyone's names at the table jotted down. John suddenly felt ill. Dean suggested they all go start the dancing. The DJ played Wham's "Careless Whisper." John half-heartedly stumbled through the song. It was hardly 11 p.m. but Charming needed to leave. Excuses were made. He drove Mom home in silence and refused to stay, even though midnight was only minutes away. She was confused, but that was typical.

I had spent the night at Jackie's. When Mom woke up the next morning, she tried calling Charming at home. His mother said he was probably at his office. She sounded worried. Mom was also worried about what Charming might be doing at his office. She called, he answered. He didn't want to talk. She got in the car and started driving to his office. On the way, "Careless Whisper" played on the radio. The night before had been the first time she had heard it. She started listening to words. She particularly was struck by the phrase "guilty feet ain't got no rhythm." She couldn't help but wonder if Kathy had set the whole thing up. Arriving at Charming's office, he confessed that he was still seeing the "girlfriend" because she thought that he loved her and was afraid of what she would do to herself if she saw him in the newspaper with my mother. Disgusted, Mom walked out, picked me up from Jackie's and put our house up for sale.

CODA

In May, our house sold. We moved back into the condo I had known as a child (our tenants having just been kicked out for dealing drugs, which might help to explain the ghostly visitations they had of my great grandmother). I'd finish up the school year and we'd find a new house, sell the condo, and move on.

Then, the doorbell rang and Mom found Charming standing on her doorstep. He had gone to the old house and found it empty. The following Sunday, he went to our old bishop to ask where we had gone. He was apologetic. Mom said she needed to pick me up from school. He wanted to stay. She said I didn't need to see him. And I never did.

EMAIL EXCERPT: A NEW LIFE, IN A NEW TOWN

I decided that it was time to move. We needed to get away from the past and the pity and move to a normal neighborhood. We sold the house and moved to Sandy in July of 1985.

You seemed to adjust well and did well at Silver Mesa. Marilyn Turner took care of you before and after school and you and Matt became good friends. Adam Turner would baby-sit you. I dated Doug and though he had some real problems he kept me away from John and you seemed to get along.

A DIFFERENT PLACE, ANOTHER LIFE

Doug was a substitute teacher who enjoyed the outdoors. We'd often go cross-country skiing together, which was a change of pace from the downhill skiing I was doing with my cousins on the weekends when Mom worked. Like most children, I was fairly reckless when it came to racing down mountains. I wasn't so much fearless, as I was simply too naïve to realize that black-diamond runs at top speed weren't exactly the safest of options. I had my share of crash landings and near-run-ins with trees, but made it through without injury.

Because skiing typically happened on Saturday, there was always the temptation of skipping out on church the following morning. Since turning eight years old, Mom never forced me into attending. She'd simply tell me to pray about it and if I felt like I didn't need to go, then I didn't have to go. I always went, partly because I knew she'd be disappointed if I didn't, and also because it seemed like the right thing to do. I liked going to church and took it as seriously as any kid ever could. I wasn't exactly pious, but I was, for the most part, well-behaved.

During weekdays, when not in school, I spent my time at the Turner's house. They had a handful of kids, including Matt, who was my age. For better or worse, there aren't any scandalous tales to be told about my time there. We'd play football in the backyard, watch movies, or draw complex fortresses armed to the hilt with machine-gun turrets, missile launchers, and secret escape routes.

During this period, my right foot became seriously infected and black lines shot up my leg. It was determined that there were fragments of glass imbedded beneath the arch of my foot. This led to a handful of visits to Dr. Thomas' office that were dominated by my screaming, terrifying those in the waiting room, while he tried to remove the objects causing the infection. For weeks, I spent most of the day soaking my foot in water. The infection subsided and Dr. Thomas, who was as traumatized by my visits to his office as I was, took me to the circus with his family as a peace offering. We had Happy Meals on the way with Chicken McNuggets; I was more of a hamburger kid, but all was forgiven.

GLASNOST

Caught adrift in 1996, I washed ashore on the remnants of Joyce's Dublin. I'd lost my mind mid-winter and went overseas in spring to find it. At my side was Hillary, my Hermione Granger, the dearest and smartest of friends. She knew a thing or two about my predisposition for madness and kept me around regardless. It was her family who provided a temporary sanctuary following high school graduation when I gave into temptation and dyed my hair electric red like songsmith Miki Berenyi. Mom disapproved.

Dublin—I remember the overwhelming kindness, the glow of pubs during post-dusk wanderings, the small rooms, the River Liffey, and seeing *Millennium Approaches*, the first half of Tony Kushner's two-part play, *Angels in America: A Gay Fantasia on National Themes*.

Angels in America captured a sense of the horror and fear that came with the AIDS epidemic from the perspective of the gay community. It was celebrated and reviled as high art and blasphemous trash; it mixed the beauty of religious metaphor and iconography with a bawdy and coarse narrative.

It was a phenomenon that dominated the theater landscape for the better part of the 1990s and forced its way into the mainstream conversation.

At the heart of the play is the story of Joe Pitt, a closeted gay Mormon, and his wife Harper.

This plot point inevitably bound me to the play in a way that would eventually become a burden. Meanwhile, its reach was so ubiquitous that it was an easy reference point I could lean on as I searched for my own voice and opinion regarding my father. The world had embraced Kushner's fiction, maybe someday it would accept my truth.

My life: it was something like a famous work of art. Only it wasn't. It wasn't at all. I just didn't know that yet.

The curtain opens, angel descends, the curtain falls and I begin to boil over.

Kushner failed to play tribute to the ferocity of my mother. Harper, caught between hallucinatory voyages to Antarctica and the heartache of being married to a discreetly gay man whose closet door had been ripped from its hinges, was weak and fragile. She lacked any semblance to my mother.

I didn't even consider that my father might be found somewhere between Kushner's prose. Was he there in the shadows of the trees or in the play's final crescendo before everything goes dark? I wasn't prepared to begin that journey.

NOT THE KARATE KID

Twice a week, my name was Ryan Pointer. While the misunderstanding might seem insignificant, it seemed to symbolize my place in life: always one letter short of right. It was fourth grade, a new house in a new town, the traditional, symbolic move from one stage of life into another by actually picking up and moving.

I'm tiny, smaller than my age or even stature would suggest. Not damaged, but somehow diminished as I stand nervously dressed in a white gi (typical karate outfit, not nearly as interesting as a ninja getup but you take what you can get). My cousin Scott is somewhere in the room with a matching ensemble but my eyes are focused on the instructor as he demonstrates a sweeping kick, knocking over one of my fellow classmates.

Downstairs, mothers are Jazzercising away to a-ha while we trained to be masters of self-defense. Unfortunately, it was slightly more traditional than what was depicted in *The Karate Kid*. No "wax on, wax off" or trying to catch flies with chopsticks. Learning karate wasn't nearly as much fun as pretending to be a ninja. You had to punch from your waist and swivel your hips when you kicked, and back flips weren't part of the rudimentary course. It didn't help that our instructor was some Caucasian guy with a bad mustache who couldn't ever get my name right.

Despite my inner belief that I would prove myself a kung fu prodigy, I wasn't particularly adept at karate. I enjoyed going; it gave me something to do and was better than sitting in a corner trying to read a book while a wild herd of mothers danced around to last year's pop hits. I only really lost interest when Scott received his orange belt before I did.

I had missed the opportunity to get my yellow belt when Scott got his. I figured I could take Scott in a bar room brawl and somehow that gave me a yellow belt by default. Unfortunately, the judges didn't agree with my philosophy.

"Ryan Pointer, you signed up for an orange but I think you meant to sign up for yellow—which you've earned."

And he moved down the list. Scott received his orange. I might have been bitter; I was discouraged. Clearly, it was time to find a new hobby.

SAVING CHRISTMAS

Not wanting to repeat the scene from the year before, I made it quite clear early on to my mother that I was going to be getting a present for her that year. I had her drive me to Fred Meyer and told her to wait in the car. I had purchased many things without a parent to walk me through the process and had always taken a certain amount of joy in my independence. Nonetheless, I had yet to grasp the notion of sales tax. I had seen the vacuum in an advertisement and had heard my mother talk about how nice it would be to have a small handheld vacuum. It was in my price range, $19.99 or thereabouts. While I can't give you the exact details of the transaction, I remember the moment quite vividly (although it plays out in my head as if I were an audience member and not a participant). I simply walked up to pay, didn't have enough, and without any sort of scene, the woman behind me simply offered up some change to cover the difference. It was a monumental moment for me, but not because a woman helped me; I thought that's what adults were supposed to do. I had often seen my mother offer kindness to strangers. It was monumental, because for the first time I felt like I was really giving my mother a surprise that she would like.

Returning to the car, Mom asked how things had gone. I told her I didn't have enough money but a nice lady in the store had helped me make up the difference.

> When I opened up the hand vacuum on Christmas Day I was crying not only because Ryan had picked it out himself but that some lady had realized how important it was to him and helped him realize his dream and his independence. I always rush to help anyone in need at the check stand because of the kindness of one woman.

SLIVERS OF LIGHT

It's sometime after 5 p.m., the light of early evening pouring through the long blinds on the glass sliding door. It is summer, the carpet is warm as it scratches and rubs my cheek. Mom's a shout away in the kitchen making dinner. I'm trying to ignore the firestorm of words coming from the television. It's too late; I've been pulled from the Neighborhood of Make-Believe.

It is the mid '80s and a mix of fear and occasional information dominates the nightly news regarding this devastating acronym, AIDS. Most of the words remain the same: "homosexuals," "unprotected sex," "needle sharing," "blood transfusions," and "no cure in sight." How long had I known that my father had died from AIDS? I always knew. So why not just say it aloud?

"That's what my dad died of."

We were in a new world, not starting over, but starting fresh. My father was a half-kept secret and I always knew why. It didn't need to be avoided anymore.

"If they ask you how your father died, you don't have to tell them AIDS. You can tell them your father died of pneumonia."

Pneumonia: the colloquial cover to obscure my scarlet letter.

MICHAEL'S GIFT

When Mom started dating Dave, I didn't think much of it. He was a nice enough person, far better than Charming and that's all that really mattered. I don't remember spending much time with him, although I'm sure we did and those occasions have simply meshed in with the years' worth of memories. In late May of 1987, Mom married David and became Patti Lamb.

This marriage, which took place in the Provo LDS Temple, effectively gave my mother the life she had always wanted, but the path was made difficult by my father's refusal to sever the bond that existed between them. In order to marry David and be bound to him forever, the sealing to my father would have to be broken.

Because my father was dead, the process was far more complicated. My mother's request would be taken before the leadership of the church and they'd decide if there were grounds to break the sealing. She was warned that it was doubtful, despite the circumstances, that her request would be granted. Yet, it was granted, and without the expected struggle. Mom believes that my father, by spirit or otherwise, reached out and gave his consent and relinquished his bond to her.

UNDERSTANDING THE DIFFERENCE

In the editing, organizing, and rewriting of my mother's recollections, it became increasingly difficult to find any of the father I remember in his behavior. I could understand the self-loathing grief, the suffering, and even the deceit, but not the cruelty that he offered my mother in exchange for wedding vows. I couldn't imagine ever loving my father fully ever again. She could forgive him; but the deeper I dug, the less I believed that I would be able to.

Mom feared when I grew older that I, when faced with my father's sexuality, would reject him. This was, in part, why she kept him in my life as much as possible. Two decades of ignorance, blind rhetoric, and bitter opinion hadn't shaken my love for my father. The way he had hurt my mother was something entirely different.

In March of 2008, I was holed up in a house in Croydon, England just outside of London. Black Rebel Motorcycle Club, the band I was working for at the time, was on a brief tour hiatus. I had been writing for days, sessions that would often start in the early afternoon and stretch deep into the night and in the silence of my isolation, I spiraled into a shouting match with God, refusing to continue writing if the cost was my love for my father. One of us did the shouting. The other listened. Then, it was my turn to listen as I was left in the silence of my own thoughts. Who was my father? I don't really know. He was a man, not a creature that should be spoken of only in whispers, if ever at all.

I think we are all asked to sacrifice a part of ourselves to find our place in this life. Maybe my father could not part with what he felt was asked of him. Then again, maybe he gave up his dream so that Mom and I might have ours. All I know is that when he left Mom, he made certain that he hadn't destroyed our lives and showered us with an affection that he never gave to himself. He refused to live a lie, even if that meant losing all the comforts that he had in the world. It might seem like the smallest of gestures, but to Mom and me it makes all the difference.

LAUGHTER

I'm forty-two years old, sitting at the kitchen table with my mother, my aunt Cheryl (who is visiting from Denver), and my father's high school friends Steve and Kay. Someone has commented on how serious my father was all of the time. I'm explaining that initially one of the motivations behind writing about my childhood was to find a memory of my father laughing.

"Did you find one?" Steve asks because he can't remember one of his own.

"Yes, I did."

It's Friday night; Dad, Bryan, and I are in the warm yellow glow of the den. The television is on but none of us are watching. I'm scribbling my way through a series of impressionistic landscapes, while Bryan and my father fold laundry. Dad holds up a pair of Bryan's boxer briefs and begins to mock them. I can laugh because my collection of superhero and cartoon themed underoos has made me an undergarment expert. Bryan spars back with a comment about my father's choice in underwear fashion. They're laughing, we're all laughing.

It isn't until I'm half-way through the telling of the story that I realize that Steve and Kay may not be comfortable imagining my father folding underwear with his boyfriend. It's a scene that must feel a million miles removed from the memories they have of him.

It is the most real and at ease that I remember my father being. I don't see this memory as much as I feel it. It's mundane and that's why it is beautiful.

STRANGERS WHEN WE MEET

After interviewing my father's family and friends in late 2018 and early 2019, I was forced to confront and reassess old stories with the new details I'd been given. I was a decidedly different person than the young man who shook his fist and locked himself away in Croydon. I'd written a book; I didn't know what it was about anymore.

I was angrier. Frustration left me rudderless; I was adrift. I didn't like what I had learned about my father's childhood. I was more cognizant of how I had allowed the opinions of the world to influence the way that I saw my father. I felt broken—incapable of moving forward and impossible to repair.

When Grandpa Bob told me that there were things that he left out of his story, he didn't have to explain. I knew exactly what he had left out. I was disappointed, but not surprised.

Bob and Gloria were alive when the first two drafts of this book were written. They knew I was writing it; Mom made sure of that. I couldn't raise the courage to ask any questions and they didn't freely offer any answers.

When I was a child, I didn't know there were things that needed to be said. As I grew older, I thought keeping quiet was more respectful.

There was also fear.

Plenty of people who didn't know my father had terrible things to say about him. I was afraid that those who knew him would be equally disparaging—their opinions harder to ignore.

I've come to regret my silence.

What if Bob and Gloria were looking for a safe place to talk about their son? When Bob pulled me aside, was he trying to open a door that in my short-sightedness I slammed shut? Did he too need reassurance? Who else could he talk to? How different would have life been for all of us, if we could have mourned together without the burden of shame? What stories could we have told? What love could we have shared?

THEN THERE WAS HE

I had never expected my mother to remarry. I wasn't opposed to the idea, or I didn't think I was, as much as I couldn't imagine what life would be like with a full-time father figure in the house. It had always been the two of us with the occasional guest appearance by whomever we happened to let in. Following the wedding, we moved into David's house in North Salt Lake. Both houses had been put up for sale but ours sold quite quickly; there seemed to be little interest in Dave's. It was quite easily the loneliest summer of my life.

By the time school started in the fall, I had put on a considerable amount of weight. Most of my days had been spent playing computer games, watching films or television. My physical activity was limited to running around in the backyard with a squirt gun, fighting off the imaginary evils that surrounded me. It was always me, just me, alone.

At school, I was slow to make friends. North Salt Lake is essentially a large hill covered in houses. Dave's was at the top, school was at the bottom. Each morning, I would walk down the winding streets that weaved back and forth. One morning, I took a shortcut, stumbled and tore a sizable hole in the knee of my pants. Mom was already at work, there would have been no one at home to sympathize or mend what was broken. I was terrified by what my classmates would think. Positive or negative, I didn't want the attention. Arriving at school, I took some scotch tape and mended the pants as best as I could.

The entire day, I worried that the tape wouldn't hold and that at some point, the cracks would begin to show. My mother's marriage, the one thing that she always wanted, left me feeling vulnerable and entirely alone.

Mom would eventually convince Dave to move back into the neighborhood in Sandy, only two or three blocks away from where we lived before. Soon I had a sister, Kathryn, and then another, Melanie. Unfortunately, whatever snapped inside of me following my mother's remarriage never fully healed and I drifted into adolescence, unprepared for what waited for me. My father's sexuality hadn't meant much to me as a child, but as my teens approached, it became another point of weakness. I wasn't gay, a thousand years in the presence of my father or his friends wouldn't have changed that, but I felt that my father's identity had become interwoven with mine. I was living his secrets, as well as mine. I watched from a distance as AIDS was demystified and the gay community transformed from a poorly kept secret into something mainstream society would have to acknowledge. For years, the world tried to distort my father. I was told that he was beyond redemption, that he had chosen his sexual orientation like an alcoholic picks his addiction. They hadn't known my father. I had and I knew better.

Still, when Mom told me that she feared that there might come a day when I would reject my father, I had to consider that as a possibility. I've questioned myself for decades, never expecting to find any kind of answer.

Here, at the age of forty-three, more than thirty-five years after his death (a stretch of time longer than Dad's life), I've begun to find peace.

I did not deny my love for him in his absence; I would have never abandoned it in his presence.

THE SPIRAL STAIRCASE

It is said and believed that my father, not long after his death, visited his younger sister Sherry. She was attending a session in an LDS temple when he approached her and asked that she give comfort to the family; he was fine. When she failed to pass on the message, he visited her again and repeated his request.

This moment is woven into the history of the Painter family. They all reference it in our conversations.

There was never any question in my mind. If there is a heaven, my father is in it.

I dreamt of a white house, immaculate and smooth. Standing in a foyer bathed in light, I am approached by a man. The light emanates from him, a hot, burning white glow that illuminates and obscures him from my view. I cannot see his face, only his outstretched hand as he leads me to a spiral staircase. I follow him. My legs are long, not those of a little boy. I am myself, but older. Along the walls as we ascend are photographs. There are images of days familiar and events that I do not recognize. There, I am as a young boy and then as an older boy, a young man. My lifetime laid out before me and the sudden understanding that my father would be given the chance to watch me grow as he sits on one side of the looking glass and I on the other. It is a lonely comfort, a consolation, but also a promise and an eternal truth that he would never truly leave me to face life on my own.

AFTERWORD

EMERGING FROM THE RABBIT HOLE

Sir Jonathan Miller, commenting on his BBC production of *Alice in Wonderland*, said something that sums up my childhood perfectly: "In the middle of the dream you scarcely notice that it is bizarre. It is only by hindsight that you think how odd to have experienced or thought or visualized all that."

For it seemed to me, that the quality of my childhood was that in the middle, I scarcely noticed that it was bizarre. Yes, there were challenges, but mostly there was love and compassion.

Writing this book has forced me to abandon the imagined history that I created for my parents. I wanted to uncover a story where there was romance and a house with a white picket fence and perfectly manicured people to match the perfectly manicured lawn.

There was no house or love that would have made us a storybook family. It was naïve of me to think that there ever could have been. Still, there was love. Not a conventional love, but a love all the same. We couldn't stand failing so we simply did the best we could with what we were given.

I am deeply saddened by how little I know of my father. I miss the conversations we never had. I regret not knowing more of his side of the story. His insight. His truth. I am grateful that my mother allowed me to know him at all. In the cool quiet of his absence, I make do with the warmth of love that radiates from these few memories.

Thank you, Mom, for being strong enough to do what you felt was right and never giving up on your dreams, no matter how unattainable they seemed. You are my hope when I have none. You are all that I could ever strive to be. Thank you for teaching me that when in doubt, love, because it is love that will truly set you free.

ABOUT THE AUTHOR

Ryan lives in Salt Lake City
surrounded by paper and plastic.

Made in the USA
Middletown, DE
29 October 2020